Turning Your Why? Into Why Not?!

Navigating Human Existence

Rev. Sheree Taylor-Jones

TURNING YOUR WHY? INTO WHY NOT!

First edition. July 25, 2019.

Copyright © 2019 Sheree Taylor-Jones.

ISBN 978-1689399982

Written by Sheree Taylor-Jones.

Dedicated to:

Graham, a man I couldn't have even imagined existed, yet I have the pleasure of calling you my husband, my partner, my friend, and my playmate. Thank you for supporting me and reminding me of my fabulousness when at times I had forgotten. Your love, kindness, and graciousness are a blessing to my soul. I'm a better person because of you. What's our next adventure?!

With Gratitude:

- Rev. Greg Cole, thank you for your soulful support and being a person of love and integrity. I am so blessed to call you friend. The comedic moments we share in life are priceless!
- Rev. Dr. Martha Creek, thank you for reminding me that I am free to be my truest expression and all of me is vital.
- Sharon Dwyer, LUT, I appreciate your authenticity and being my major cheerleader, you never faltered in believing in me. Thank you for your feedback as a beta reader, I treasure your thoughts.
- Rev. Linda Machesic, I am changed by your encouragement and support now and most importantly when I started on this new pathway ten years ago.
- Mary Beth Mincey, BFF extraordinaire, it has been a long 30 year journey. You and your family are my family. Glyn, Amanda, Stephanie thank you for adopting me in your hearts.

- Rev. Paulette Pipe, I appreciate you being my possibilities and ex-patriate partner.
- Rev. Dr. Karren Scapple, thank you for your support during seminary. I appreciate your friendship and see you as a light in the Unity Movement. LUS
- Mikayla Schmitz, you blew me away with your insights, feedback, and suggestions as a beta reader! Are you ready to be the phenomenal woman I already see?
- Unity of Lawrence for being the exact community you needed to be and for allowing me to evolve with you.
- All the Divine No answers that have inspired and guided me.

Thank you, the reader for your willingness to look at yourself with new eyes of Love. You are a powerful co-creator and I'm grateful that you are choosing to be awakened and be the Light you want to see in the world.

Table of Contents

Introduction

The purpose of this book is to help you become comfortable about questioning yourself, your beliefs, and your ideology. Purpose-filled lives require us to occupy a consciousness of questioning our culture, society, and the established systems that we operate within as we inhabit this plane of existence. Self-actualization demands that we discern if the beliefs we hold are our truths or the truths of our parents and society. Becoming self-aware means we are fearless in questioning areas that may have been considered taboo, such as our understanding of God and human sexuality.

This work asks us to look at long held beliefs we may hold about ourselves and others, while being willing to ask the tough questions such as, "Are my beliefs true?" "Whose belief is this?" "Who told me this was truth and why do I continue to believe this?" "What would it mean if I created my own beliefs?" The Socratic quote, "The *unexamined life is not worth living*" is a powerful statement to the journey to self-awareness, spiritual enlightenment, and freedom from oppression.

My hope in this modern-day tale of trauma and over-coming resistance to what is, you will find useful tools in which to examine your own life. This is a daring call to your life's purpose by your willingness to look at life's stresses, injustices, confusions, and difficulties in a new way that allows you to find fulfillment and peace once again. This means you will also have an opportunity to look at your unconscious biases, we all have them – yes even me, discern what biases you have, decide which ones you choose to release, and which ones you keep.

The goal of this book is to help you remember your Truth again. Your Truth is that you are a Divine human being. Life's experiences have a way of making us forget this Truth. My purpose is to remind you through real-life experiences that you too can live in this world as your Truth in a more peace-filled and loving way led by Spirit.

Chapter 1

"Why?" Child Defies God

We are born and we die. Everything in-between is change. We spend so much of our time resisting change. Even holding on to the past when the past is painful and no longer serves us. But we find comfort in knowing that pain. We know what it feels like and what to expect from that pain. This was how I lived the first thirty years of my life.

My badge of honor in life: I'm a strong woman who is a survivor. A survivor of trauma, survivor of re-created trauma, and Olympic medalist in pain endurance. How could I see myself any other way? It is from our own life experiences that we see and interact with people. It's from our perception of good and evil, right and wrong, love and hate that we view others' words and actions. We compare our lives to theirs, and come up with either scenario: they have had a charmed life, while our own life has been hell, or we are better than them and they are unworthy. Yet, we have no idea what their walk and journey has been. We just react to their words or actions gleaned from our self-conceived ideas.

Truth: You create your own heaven or your own hell—no one else, nothing else. There is no one persecuting, dishonoring, or disrespecting you more than you. We live at a time when we are trying to make sense of a world that seems to no longer make sense. In our humanity we want to figure out why people do and say the things they do. Why is this happening? Why...?

I too started my life as a "Why?" child. *Why is the sky blue? Why do I have to eat vegetables? Why is red, red? Why are kids so mean?* I remember my mom saying to me in frustration, "If you ask me *why* one more time, I will scream." At the time I thought Mom didn't know the answers and this was her way of dealing with me. I was about five years old at the time and knew my mission was to find the answers.

When I was a child, I would have mystical experiences with Jesus. I didn't realize at the early age of five that I was astral projecting my spirit out of my body to commune with God. If you are wondering how I could do such a thing as such an early age, the answer is trauma. Astral projection became a way for me to feel safe during traumatic times in my early childhood. My parents fought violently when they were married, but it didn't seem to become vicious until we moved from England and started living in the United States. I think the stress of the change to American culture became too much. But as they fought, especially at night, I would leave my body and speak with God. Each time I was bathed in love and comfort. Each time I would beg to stay and be told it wasn't my time. Each time I was told I would be okay and I needed to return.

As a young child I loved the mysteries of the Universe; I was excited by knowing there was "someone up there" who cared about me; to me, it was a real relationship. It wasn't until my indoctrination by my family that things changed. My family raised me in a very conservative religious upbringing, where one followed the rules to be worthy of God. But there was a secret. My mom and my gran were also practicing Obeah. You may ask, "What is Obeah?" I found an article entitled "6 Types of Witches from Around the World" at the website, Mental Floss that had a simple explanation of Obeah:

> "As a folk magic-religion hybrid, Obeah flourished
> in the West Indies during the slave trade largely as
> a force of resistance. The dark magic uses spells to
> make predictions, gain knowledge, or obtain

assistance for any task. While Obeah isn't a religion in the sense that there is any sort of established church or ceremonies, female and male practitioners are seen as spiritual guides that can help with any number of problems."

This practice is done on an individual basis and has no creed but is often syncretized with Christianity. In my home life, Obeah was hidden, couldn't be mentioned to anyone, and if it was spoken about, it was spoken in codes. The secrecy comes from the persecution of those who practiced it during times of slavery. As Christianity was forced into the culture of enslaved people, Obeah was condemned as black magic. So it was known in our home that Christian churches would frown on this practice.

To create even more chaos in my comprehension of the world, I was educated at a private grammar school in a Catholic community, which led to my being baptized and then confirmed as a Catholic. The teachings were so opposed to the secrets that were going on at home that I often felt confused and anxious. I learned in Catholic school about a magical, all-powerful, and vengeful God. I was sure this God would smite my family down. When that didn't occur, I did the best I could to ignore any witchcraft going on in the home.

While in complete contradiction, at least in my mind, my family still used the Bible as a tool to force their ideologies on me. As I grew up, Catholicism became ingrained as my own belief system, and I came to fear God. This concept of God stayed with me until I was in my late twenties, when I started to individuate. Once I started to challenge the Catholic teachings, I became really angry at God, and if anyone asked me about my religion, I would say I was a recovering Catholic.

My relationship with God had become so difficult that I decided I was not even going to have a conversation, furthermore, a relationship, to a deity that could be so cruel. I had numerous crises of faith, until I had no faith; I was just this rage-filled person, angry with a punishing God. At this stage of my spiritual development, my concept of God was a powerful superman on the throne in heaven. I was furious with God; I felt that "he" was punishing me unnecessarily. After all, I was a nerd and geek girl: A+ student, no drugs, no sex, no smoking.

As I embraced adulthood, navigating the world was filled with hardships. I'm a good person and didn't deserve to be enduring such hardships. In my mind my questions continued: *What kind of God would allow me to be born into an abusive family? What kind of God would allow me to marry an alcoholic, who was unfaithful and a bigamist? What kind of God would take my unborn baby? What kind of God would allow me to be a widow at the age of twenty-six when the alcoholic husband died of acute alcohol intoxication? What kind of God would force me to file for bankruptcy because said husband committed financial fraud?* I was enraged with this kind of God. I also hated the Bible, and felt it was written by men abusing their power and authority. I had been Bible-thumped by my family and ministers for too many years.

Fast-forward twenty years and my "why practice" was making me a very unhappy person. My questions of why were rarely answered with satisfaction; if anything, I became more cynical and despairing of a world filled with immoral, corrupt, narcissistic, rage-fueled human beings. I wanted off this planet now. I was filled with depression and would have been relieved to die. I wasn't technically suicidal, but I had ideations of not living, of not waking up in the morning, of possibly getting killed by someone (painlessly, of course) so I wouldn't have to deal with this world anymore. I felt this way because my interpretations of the ways of the world were unconscionable and I couldn't find answers that were satisfying or Truth.

One of my mentors and friend Martha Creek has a saying, "*Why* is the road to hell!" When I first heard that statement I howled with laughter; there is a simple truth in that statement. I thought of all the times I asked the question why. My reasoning behind the question included: to understand others, to know truths, to find answers, to find a reason for being, to explain the unexplainable, to feel comfortable in my own skin. Hmm, after laughing at the statement "*Why* is the road to hell!" I became annoyed, and then got ticked off because "asking why" was my practice in navigating a world that didn't make sense to me into one that could make sense.

GOD HUMBUG

What kind of God who is omniscient and omnipotent would allow all this suffering? In my indoctrinated understanding, it was an awful God, a God not worthy of my praise or adoration. So began my separation and justified anger with a deity that possessed no compassion for us mortals. *I'll show God*, I thought. *I don't need him, and my life will be so much better under my own control.* I believed life was hard and unfair. But I also believed I could overcome any hardship if I continued working and striving for a better life, have a home, and eventually create my own family. That's the dream we all are told we must achieve to be acknowledged as successful. Who needs God for that?

Yet, as I continued living, I felt not whole in my life, something significant was missing. I tried to live my life with dignity and kindness to others, but I felt lost and so alone even when with other people. This set me on a journey of discovery. I think it's the wisdom of our souls that creates this feeling of discontent to push us to awaken. In my spiritual search I experienced, practiced, and embraced many religions and traditions. I studied many different Christian religious sects, which included Baptist, Methodist, Pentecostal, Jehovah Witnesses, Seventh-day Adventist, and then explored nondenominational Christian ministries. I also delved into the other two Abrahamic faiths, Judaism and Islam. Imagine my surprise at discovering that each of the three religions Islam, Judaism, and Christianity originate from the same place, through Abraham's sons. I'm shocked at how much violence, damage, ethnic cleansing mankind has engaged in on behalf of the "right religion."

In my spiritual journey, I unearthed there is an overriding hierarchy of patriarchy that underpins each of those religions. This led me to ask myself what was before the Abrahamic religions. I then became a Wiccan practitioner for many years, embracing the Divine feminine and rituals. I later delved into studying Eastern religions, such as Buddhism and Hinduism.

My journey into self-actualization included coming to the awareness that I had experienced childhood abuse, and discovering patterns of behavior in my adult relationships that were attempts to heal my childhood. Part of my self-renewal was individuating and owning myself, as well as learning to make better choices in relationships. Yet, something vital was still missing; I was still having an unfulfilled intellectual relationship with God, and my search for a new understanding of God commenced again.

Eventually, in the late eighties I found Unity, a transdenominational spiritual community built on New Thought principles and ideology. I started at the Unity in New York City, with the Reverend Eric Butterworth. The messages were transformational, and I loved it there. As my spiritual life became richer, I transcended religious dogma. My life started to shift and flourish. I felt hopeful about life and looked forward to new positive things coming into my life. I remember thinking people should know about another way to see God, through the lens of love and goodness. This was the first time I thought it would it be cool to share this with others.

But it took me another thirty years in the wilderness before I came to realize my purpose is to help others find a new way of seeing God, while facilitating a safe space to allow individuals to shift consciousness and live as the frequency of Love in the world. As I look back on those wilderness years, it would be easy to label those years as wasted time and missed opportunities, but in reality I came to realize that those wilderness years were blessings, not failures.

I won't lie to you and tell you God whispered in my ear, "Sheree, you will be a Unity minister," and I said, "Yippee." Nope, in my human wisdom, I ran for many years. I had all these rational thoughts about why I couldn't go into ministry, such as my professional career was vital and necessary to make money to support myself. But the career of my intellect blocked my Divine truth, my life purpose. You see under all that logic was a belief that was untrue: I wasn't worthy enough. I believed that I was without power to manifest a world that can work for all beings.

Becoming a minister at this late time in my life—I started seminary in 2013 at the age of fifty—allowed me to do the healing and deep self-awareness work necessary to be a new kind of minister. I am a minister who sees each person as the Divine incarnated, therefore, worthy and valued. Many of us have experienced or heard of ministers that have burnt out, damaged congregants, divided ministries. If I had become a minister twenty or thirty years ago, I could have easily become one of those ministers because I didn't have the maturity, wisdom, and grace that I do today. So I have a sense of gratitude for my experiences and lives lived.

How did I go from being angry and having no relationship with God to becoming a minister? To be honest, having a relationship or not having a relationship with God is really about my understanding of what God is and is not. Being raised in Catholicism, my concept of God was that of an omnipotent male deity who sat on a throne in the celestial realm. He was an old white male with a long, white mane of hair that flowed into an equally white beard. He would have a staff in one hand and a big black book in the other hand that held the name of each person written with that person's deeds of good and evil.

Depending on how much good the person did to outweigh their sins would determine what was in store for that person's soul. This God had many superpowers such as: x-ray vision—he could see through walls and roofs, so you always had to be careful about what you were doing or saying; he was also a mind reader, and he would know your thoughts of lust, greed, envy, and you would be judged based on those thoughts, you didn't even have to take action. He had power over all the elements, so he could kill you with flood or fire; he even controlled all the animals on land or in the sea, just look at the story of Jonah and the whale.

Contrary to this past and erroneous belief system, I have come to recognize that as a human being, I am here on this planet to have all human experiences, not to hide from a deity all that I am. Yes, experiences such as joy and happiness, but also those experiences that previously would have been perceived as "sinful." Because of my religious upbringing, in the past any relationship I had with God would be fear-filled because I considered myself living against God's laws. From the moment I engaged in sex without marriage, I believed I was doomed.

This God, of my limited understanding, could see my sexual acts and hear my lust-filled thoughts; I was waiting for any day to be smote down. The teachings and ultimately my belief in this vengeful God meant God would never forgive me, and I was going to go to purgatory at the minimum, but hell was probably my destination if I continued down this path. Eventually God became this deity that I had to avoid at all costs. I couldn't have a conversation with him because I knew he was sooo disappointed in me.

In this journey, I discovered that it is our human need to define God in a particular way and to give God qualities that mankind understands is how we limit the totality and boundlessness of God. It's in our definition that we create the illusion of a God who is separate and without compassion. If we define God as a supreme being who controls our lives and destiny, then each of us would be waiting to be saved. In this belief system, the best-case scenario is that God as "Superman" would stop the things we deem as bad from happening to us. And when God does not stop them from happening to us or stop the hatred in the world, we are quick to blame God.

What if in mankind's drive for answers to the unknowable, the indefinable, we have made an error in our understanding of what God is? What if God is simply the unlimited energy of Love, Life, and Light? What if this unlimited energy is in everything, including you and me? Then would we continue to blame God, or would we embrace being responsible for saving ourselves and our brothers and sisters.

What if the reality is each person is born with Divine consciousness, God, inside each of us? What if each of us incarnates to evolve and know the truth of what we are, while our physical bodies exist as vehicles to express our consciousness? And while we are on this planet, we have the capacity to learn, explore, shift, transform, and love ourselves as well as others. Most importantly, we discover that we are all connected through our divinity, our spiritual essence.

Of course, we all have choices as to whether we grow in consciousness or choose to stay asleep to the truth of what we are, divinity. Many of us choose not to awaken to that truth. *It is in humanity's choice to stay asleep that atrocities can happen.* When we forget our truth and embrace fear, our thoughts become consumed by lack and separation. We, in turn, manifest error and hatred. You see, it's never been about holding God accountable. The responsibility and accountability are strictly ours. The most powerful way we can facilitate this shift in consciousness is to behold the Divine within each person, while walking the talk. There is no "us versus them." There is no "I'm right and you're wrong." There is no blame, no shame, no guilt.

The author of the Gospel of Mark writes in chapter 12, verses 30-31, "You shall love the lord your God with all your heart, and with all your soul, and with all your mind, and with all your strength. The second is this, You shall love your neighbor as yourself. There is no other commandment greater than these."

What this means is we have two precepts to live our lives by. First precept: If God is Love, Life, and Light, and is within us, then this is about loving ourselves in totality. Love is our primary purpose as a spiritual being. Everything we are, everything we do, and everything we think needs to come from love. Second precept: We are to be in loving service to each other led by Spirit. There is no other law.

So when you hear a fellow human being struggling with emotions or lacking consciousness, love them, listen to them, hold the high watch for them—holding the high watch is simply knowing the truth with them, the truth is they are both Divine and human, while showing them kindness to lift them up. Then be the Divine in action by how you live your life, the words you choose, and the actions you take.

We know this Truth as very young children before indoctrination into our families or societies occurs. Very small children love everyone and everything. They are enamored with life. Think back to your earliest memories, remember what you felt and how you viewed your world.

Take a moment to jot down a few words in the boxes below to describe *your perceptions as a child*, prior to indoctrination: (Worksheet 1)

Childhood Worldview

Place one-word snapshots in any area of the picture. They are part of your treasure chest!

I remember my earliest memories, I was exuberant with joy. I was this happy, bubbling energetic mass that loved. I didn't recognize differences in a boy or girl, adult or child, animal or inanimate. Everyone was my equal, and everyone would love me as I loved them. I would share food with the dog and then take food from the dog to munch on. There was no difference; the dog was my sibling. I would run and fall and laugh at myself and others. It was clear that I was here on this planet to experience it all. You see I wasn't conditioned yet to "fit" into society.

As a baby I still had the glow of the cosmos shining through me. I think that's why we fall in love so easily with babies. We can clearly see the spark of the Divine in that babe's eyes, when we look deeply we can see where we came from, and there is a yearning to connect to that again. As a child, my soul, essence, consciousness was still pure. I believe I still had an awareness of the energy, Love, and Light from God. It isn't until we internalize our parents' beliefs and hear their voices in our psyche telling us what it means to be a well-behaved child and act appropriately that we start to forget who we truly are.

I asked you to remember your earliest memories and emotions because those earliest awe-filled moments are what it feels like to resonate as the frequency of Love. That sense of wonder and celebration in all you do. Remember how you celebrated being able to walk, then walk without falling, then run? You were in awe of yourself because you loved yourself. You saw yourself as simply an extension of everything. From a psychological viewpoint, there was no individuation yet.

You were also in celebration of those around you. You heralded your playmate's ability to run as well. You were there to assist them if they fell or needed a hug. You saw everyone as equal, everyone matters, and everyone has value and should be celebrated. You simply understood that the world would be a better place if we all were happy and cared for. That is the frequency of Love.

Now you may scoff and think that is completely unrealistic. No one can live on this planet and be successful being the frequency of Love. I am suggesting that it is possible, and we can create a world where everyone thrives.

Chapter 2

A Perpetually Hijacked Society

We have been conditioned to believe the world I described is naïve. News, media, television, and social media have saturated our lives so much that we have learnt to fear things that are different, that are unknown. In the early part of mankind's evolution that made sense, it was a matter of survival. Eat the wrong vegetation, one could become ill; walk away from your village and maybe get eaten by a beast; take a wrong turn and possibly be injured.

There were no hospitals or medications to help; many things that we take for granted today would have been a life-or-death situation in the past. But that is no longer true today, and yet our primitive self still reacts to modern-day experiences as perceived life-or-death events. Our amygdala system gets hijacked, and reason flees. We then operate from our basest selves instead of our evolved self.

"If it bleeds, it leads," so said Eric Pooley of *New York* magazine back in 1989, and this has been a maxim for news reporting for decades. News reporting is not about the norm. Reporting is about the abnormal, things that shock us. Things that continue to keep us hijacked and in a state of unconscious fears. There is no logic once our amygdala is hijacked. The brain is operating completely on our emotions. When we are in this state, the thoughts and words that we allow cannot help but be negative, shaming, blaming.

It seems normal to align ourselves with people who are confirming our fears and with those who say they have a solution to those fears. Often we forget to do our own due diligence to determine if what we are being told is true. We go into agreement with those fearmongers, and perpetuate systems that are punitive and filled with injustice because it speaks to our emotionally hijacked brains.

But what happens when you stay in a constant state of survival? Your body and mind simply cannot function at its best. As for your soul, if you are fighting for your life, it's a nonstarter—it's not even relevant.

I will use some of my own past life experiences when I decided my very survival was in jeopardy as examples of being hijacked. In my first year of college, I failed calculus and physics. You may think, no big deal, just take the classes again or change majors. A simple life event. It would have been a simple life event if I hadn't been conditioned by my family, the education system, and our culture that failure is not acceptable. In my beliefs at that time, failure was simply a one-way ticket to being a homeless person. Hence, failing two core requirements for my major in engineering was the end of my life. I was on an ROTC scholarship in which I had to maintain a certain GPA and specific field of study to keep my scholarship. I was on my own. There would be no support from anyone else. I had to make it on my own.

In my mind, this was a life-or-death situation. I was so fearful that I had panic attacks and lived in an anxious state for months. I was so terrified of failure, which extrapolated into fear of my own death, I even became incapable of understanding what any teacher was instructing. I was having a "Charlie Brown" experience, all I could hear was, "Wah, wah, wah!" Holy shit! I thought I was losing my mind. My world became more and more narrow. I was working harder than ever before, and yet I was doing so poorly. You see, my amygdala was hijacked; adrenaline was coursing through my system continuously. I was fighting for my life. Without this scholarship, I couldn't finish school; without a degree I wouldn't be able to find a job to take care of myself.

Now I'm in this vicious cycle: work hard, not enough sleep or R&R, caffeine overload to keep me going, alcohol to get some sleep, and sex to be able to feel something. I finished my first year in college and knew my dreams were dead, and I would inevitably be a bag lady. You know, the woman pushing her world's belongings in a shopping cart, who is unkempt, smelly, and dirty while wearing all the clothes she owns in layers.

While I'm in this survival state, I am angry and filled with jealousy at those I perceive are making it, those less deserving or less gifted than me. I became consumed with my very existence and my desire *not* to become homeless. From this place of fear and panic I make many significant life choices that do not serve me well, such as getting married at the age of twenty.

Reactionary responses and behaviors don't serve us, and create chaos in our lives. When we are triggered to respond immediately to a given situation, we are not aligned to our wisest self. We are in our survival mode, and we don't make decisions for our highest good when we are in survival mode.

Now let's look at this life event: failing two classes. But because I believed I must continue to be a straight-A student to be worthy of success, I was unable to see this failure as a blip on life's path, as opposed to the end of my life. Where did I get this belief? I came to believe this failure was the end of my life from several of the systems that I grew up in. The first system is my family system. My family prided education above all else. I was indoctrinated from a very early age that I was the smart one; I was the one who would carry the mantle of my family's greatness. I was the firstborn in my family, which is usually the "hero" role.

The second place this belief was enforced was through the school system. In my school experiences, only the gifted and advanced students were worthy of a teacher's efforts and attention. Of course, the opposite was a fact as well; those students who behaved inappropriately also received teachers' attentions, but in a very punitive way. But I was the gifted child. I had a lot at stake from my family's and teachers' expectations. For heaven's sake, I was voted most likely to succeed in high school. The third place this belief was corroborated was through the work systems of our culture. The work system dictates those who can have good jobs versus those who cannot. In our current society, only those with a college degree are eligible to apply for a good job.

ISM LIFE IS *NOT* A FULL LIFE

I use the term *ism* to define systematic institutional biases. It is necessary to analyze our beliefs about *isms* in order to discern how we navigate in the world and to decide if we want to continue to operate in this way. I will describe a few of these isms in our society today and see which ones you currently accept as the norm and operate within.

The foundation of the Western culture is built on the "haves" and the "have-nots" being clearly defined through the process of systemic labeling via the structure of *"isms."* Classism allowed barriers to be placed between those of wealth and status and those of the masses. A clear definition for classism can be found at the website *classism.org* that states, *"Classism is differential treatment based on social class or perceived social class. Classism is the systematic oppression of subordinated class groups to advantage and strengthen the dominant class groups. It's the systematic assignment of characteristics of worth and ability based on social class."* It was understood that if you were "connected" by status or wealth, you would be allowed to attempt to create a successful life, while the masses would be in service to those elite classes.

In our recent history, indentured servitude created temporary slave-like service for the poor masses of European origins. The inception of the institution of slavery created a new classification system for people of African descent. As indentured servitude was completely eliminated by the increased importation of people into slavery, there became a clear delineation based on race. African people were not given human status, deemed inferior savages. This classification allowed them to be owned, abused, killed, and discarded. When slavery came to an end and liberty was given to those people of color, our society decided it was necessary to institute racism.

Racism is defined as prejudice, discrimination, or antagonism directed against someone of a different race based on the belief that one's own race is superior. Racism allowed barriers to be placed between those of the dominant narrative, white, and those of nonwhite races. At this time in American history, if you were a white male and didn't come from the elite classes, you would now be allowed to improve your skills through education or apprenticeships to create a life not as successful as the elite, but you and your family would thrive. If you were a man of color, these options were not available to you, but you could find a job in a service capacity or as a laborer. But most often it was the women of color who held the lion's share for keeping their families afloat by working consistently as domestic help.

Then the Equal Employment Opportunity Act in 1964 and the Equal Employment Opportunity Commission in 1972 were instituted. EEOA states it's illegal to discriminate, while the EEOC enforces the law. At the website *eeoc.gov* there is a clear description of the EEOC's responsibilities:

"The U.S. Equal Employment Opportunity Commission (EEOC) is responsible for enforcing federal laws that make it illegal to discriminate against a job applicant or an employee because of the person's race, color, religion, sex (including pregnancy, gender identity, and sexual orientation), national origin, age (40 or older), disability or genetic information. It is also illegal to discriminate against a person because the person complained about discrimination..."

This was a defining moment in which our society attempted to level the playing field. It was an understanding that all are able to work and thrive regardless of gender, identity, age, or color of one's skin. This was a conceptual upheaval to the existing work system because the law of the land stated everyone was eligible to achieve the dream. You know the dream we are all told from childhood: all one has to do is work hard, be smart and responsible, and you can have a successful life, which means a beautiful home, 2.5 children, a couple of pets, leisure time, vacations, and any material goods you desire. Finally, equality!

But the implementation of EEOA legislation seemed to have created a new need for additional barriers to be erected to keep the undesirables from success. The barrier is known as a college degree; without a college degree, many jobs were exempt from those who in the past could work their way up to success. The creation of job requirements in which a bachelor's degree was required, even if it had nothing to do with the job, instituted a new level of classism in our modern culture. I call this barrier "valuism," which suggests that if you were able to get a college degree, then you have value and can be allowed to enter the economic system to attempt success.

You may think I've created a generalization and cite an example of a computer programmer as someone who must have a degree to prove they are trained in critical thinking and understanding of coding. My response to that statement would be: does anyone need to pay $30,000 a year, which equates to $120,000 for a bachelor's degree, to learn those skills? If your answer is yes, then that means a degree becomes available to only those of wealth or giftedness. It means that it's an exclusionary requirement, especially when there are kids and adults who are brilliant programmers without the BS attached to their name.

This valuism permeates so many layers of our lives today. Without valuism, jobs that pay enough to support a family are unavailable to everyone. Without valuism, a home in a nice neighborhood is not for everyone because it's unaffordable. Without valuism, a good education isn't possible for your children because quality grammar and high school education is tied to where one's home is located.

Through these systems, family, education, culture, economic, and value, I came to believe that my life was over at nineteen years old through this one event: I failed two classes. At that time in my life, I was only able to function from my primitive self because I was in survival mode. The primitive self did not care about soul, God, others. The primitive self's only focus is on not dying and survival. This place of primitive functioning is where so many of us find ourselves after we have given up or given up on our dreams, which really equates to giving up hope. Without hope, we become lost.

Another *ism* that is economically impacting people in record numbers today is what I term: "stockism." Stockism dictates that whatever it takes to make those people who own shares of stock in a company happy is the mandate of the operations of the companies today. This equates to the value of the stocks of a company being all that matters. Via stockism, corporations and those who run corporations are only responsible to the stockholders of the company.

This has changed our economic structure so significantly that only the elite, the top one percent of our society, are able to benefit. What this translates into is that corporations will outsource work to countries with lower-wage earners, will lay off workers who have done good work in their jobs, will not offer employees benefits, will close down subsidiaries and wipe out entire towns, all in the name of ensuring stockholders are happy.

What's even more tragic, instead of corporations being accountable for the economic disaster they have created, they perpetuate a belief that there is not enough for everyone and it's someone else's fault. The blame game is at epic proportions. The corporations blame the legislature. The legislature blames the government. The government blames the individual.

Throughout this chaos, we have still been able to engineer and create wonderful tools of connection and communication known as social media. This technology enables us to finally understand that we are so similar on so many levels, no matter where we reside in the world. However, many humans have turned this gift of connectedness into away to shame, blame, and marginalize individuals. The use of social media in this way becomes an *ism*, it creates biases that negatively impact people from thriving. I call this new phenomenon "social madism." Doesn't it seem madness to use a tool of connection to bully, terrorize, and psychologically damage another human being?

Without judgment or criticisms reflect on the *isms* you just read and take personal inventory. What *isms* are you benefiting from? Which *ism* would you like to release? Which *ism* still makes sense to you and you will continue to abide by? Take a moment to go within and write your answers below: (worksheet 2)

What *isms* are mine to analyze?

BELIEF SYSTEM

All of the systems that humanity has created over time become ingrained into our own belief systems, depending on how our earliest cultural indoctrination occurred. How we are taught, raised, and developed becomes internalized in our psyche so much that we come to believe our understanding and perceptions are the right ones and, most importantly, the only ones that matter. Previously, I mentioned when we first come onto this plane of existence we are of love and light, until we are told how to fit in and behave appropriately within our society. This conditioning becomes our view of the world, it becomes our belief system.

Inherently, knowing how to navigate society and positively contribute to said society is a good thing for the individual and the group collective. It helps us all to get along together, think of it like "rules of the road." When we are driving down the road to a destination, it's vital to our survival and safety to know that most people on the road understand when to stop, yield to another vehicle, which side of the road to drive on, how fast to go, how to change lanes, etc. The rules of the road provide a way for all of us to shop, visit friends and family, travel, and much more with a relative certainty of doing this without killing ourselves or others. The problem occurs when the rules of the road become a hindrance, outdated, no longer viable, or no longer useful to us.

According to *blog.nationwide.com*, in the early 1900s there was a weird traffic rule of the road in Virginia—*"Women are prohibited from driving a car on Main Street unless her husband is walking in front of the car waving a red flag."* This rule was implemented as a means to slow down women drivers from spooking horses and killing pedestrians. Imagine if this rule was still enforced today. We would call it insanity among other things. This rule would harm lots of people today if it was still an accepted rule of the road.

Our beliefs work the same way. A belief system that made sense to our parents or grandparents may no longer be applicable for us today. But often we think that their beliefs are our beliefs because we choose not to examine them to determine if they make sense for us today. Sure, we may be willing to change how we integrate technology and scientific improvements, to create a new way of operating and being in the world. But when it comes to intangible concepts, such as God, faith, sexuality, we are less willing to examine whether our understanding and beliefs make sense, are still valid, and are even ours, or just what we have been conditioned to believe.

Once we learn how a system works and we figure out how to navigate it successfully, it's difficult to give up that particular system in which we find worth, praise, and abundance. It's human nature to want to be seen as successful. To ask us to give up a system we are successfully operating within can be seen as a threat to our very survival. We will do everything we can to uphold this system, even if it means others don't thrive. Conversely, if we put our faith into a system and we fail to navigate it successfully, we can see ourselves as worthless, a loser, or a failure. This then translates into feelings of apathy and living marginalized lives. Those who feel they are failures have simply defined themselves based on a system that someone else created and determined is necessary for humanity.

How many of us buy into the belief of others? How many of us self-destruct based on someone else's beliefs about what is worthy or has value? Right now we are seeing this self-destruction at epidemic levels because those who are in power are the ones who have successfully navigated the system, and they would rather see us self-destruct than to change a system that has proven it is broken.

Let's break down some concepts about how we operate in the world. The word paradigm has a couple of definitions, first: a framework containing the basic assumptions, ways of thinking, and methodology that are commonly accepted by members of a scientific community. The second definition of paradigm can also be used to represent a typical pattern or model of a culture, a family, business, industry, or even a community.

When I use the term paradigm, I'm using it from the perspective of the second definition while incorporating the framework of basic assumptions and thinking culturally. Paradigms come with certain attachments: this is the way we've always done it, this is the right way, and this is the accepted norm or standard. Anything that looks different is often thought of as a trial, punishment, or harassment.

Nicolaus Copernicus, a renaissance astronomer and mathematician, came to understand that the sun was the center of this solar system, as opposed to the common belief of the time, which was the Earth was the center of our solar system. His belief became heretical to the Catholic and Protestant churches. Today we would laugh at the very idea that the Earth is the center of the solar system, but for eons that was the belief and understanding. You see, it's human nature to think we are the center of all things. In time, as our scientific understanding caught up to the reality of what is, we were forced to examine that belief and change our comprehension.

Many of us have computers. We have come to realize that in order to function in our society, we must be able to operate computers quickly and effectively. When our computers slow down or don't have the memory and storage necessary to keep pace with technological advancements, we know we must upgrade. This upgrade sometimes is as simple as downloading a piece of software that can correct the errors we are experiencing.

However, there are times when we must get a whole new computer system because the old one just won't work for us. In each case we must analyze and assess what needs to be changed about our computers. In our lives, we also have to do this assessment to determine what's working, what's outdated, what needs upgrading or replacing. This analytical introspection happens by reviewing our belief systems.

What I find interesting is there is a sense of fear and terror associated with assessing our beliefs about God, faith, and who we truly are. It's as if being wrong in our previous beliefs means we are wrong. It's as if shifting our belief about God means everything else we know as truth is in jeopardy. But that is so far from the truth. It simply means we have a new awakening, a new upgrade. What If God always is, and our understanding of God evolves? For example, if God is simply Unconditional Love at all times, with all people no matter what, then the rules that humanity have created about how to be in God's favor no longer apply.

> Hildegard of Bingen, Catholic saint, author, mystic, pharmacist, composer, musician, and visionary of the twelfth century, said, "We cannot live in a world that is not our own, in a world that is interpreted for us by others. An interpreted world is not a home. Part of the terror is to take back our own listening, to use our own voice, to see our own light."

This same fearless assessment can be applied to our religious beliefs or whatever life operating system we choose to adhere to. Religion is a man-made belief system. Even the atheist has his religion, he just may not call it religion. Organized religion today has become unholy to many because its dogmas are filled with hatred, fear, and control. This is why it is imperative to analyze our beliefs about God. Our consciousness, light force, soul cannot be filled with fear and hatred and come into its wholeness. Separation is the antithesis of wholeness. Any religion that preaches of hell or damnation unless certain dictates are met cannot free our soul.

As students of Truth, we know in our greatest moments of clarity that God is Unconditional Love. The expression of pain, hurt, damnation is mankind's creation. The time to ascend from fear to embrace our highest self is now. To begin this journey to awakened awareness, I ask you, will you place your soul in charge of your journey and trust where it leads you? (Q1) That is the key to your freedom.

Imagine with me a moment, a worst-case scenario: losing one's job. This event usually creates a host of fears rising to the surface. But what if it were possible to view this event from a new awareness? The shift in awareness can be from perceiving the loss of a job as being catastrophic to having an opportunity for great change or even a learning experience. This is a type of conscious reframing, moving an issue from being a problem to it becoming an opportunity.

I've shared my own experiences with my fear of being homeless when I failed classes in college, but the same fears came up when I was laid off from my job in the banking industry. The level of anxiety and paralysis I felt was immense. I was taught to believe in the external systems of our culture; they are the authority and have all power. How could I still feel worthy when they chose to terminate my employment and no longer valued my contributions? I had to change my belief system by releasing this paradigm that no longer served me and change to a new way of being in the world.

I started to embrace the fluidity of life and celebrate that power and authority resides within me. Today I am probably on my seventh career, which led me to becoming a New Thought minister. Today I know that all things that happen are for me. Now you may not know me, but I'm not always graceful in shifts. Most times there is a WTF moment, but those moments last a very short time now, and I'm quickly ready to see how this supports me. I choose to shift in frequency. Aligning myself to Truth, I am unconditionally loved and worthy; therefore, all is for my highest good.

At those times when my energetic shift isn't graceful, my first step is to be aware of what feelings are going on within me. For example, if at first I feel fear, I feel it, acknowledge it, and don't resist it. Then I breathe, meditatively release my thoughts by focusing on my breathing, or a mantra, and sink into aligning to the frequency of God, which is Unconditional Love. From this elevated frequency, I am able to step into my wisdom and knowing. I can make decisions each time I'm aligned in Divine consciousness, and by becoming a higher vibration I transform the situation. I trust next time it will be quicker and easier to transform because I have become adept at aligning with the Divine.

We cannot be in the vibration of chaos and fear and create anew. When we vibrate in the problem, we create from the resonance of the problem, which creates different problems. We must change our vibration and frequency to the Divine to be able to create something possible that seemed impossible.

Most of our paradigms operate from us being motivated by the approval of others. To be able to transform, we have to step outside of our need for approval in order to change our frequency and our consciousness. We cannot be approval seeking and be our Divine selves—they are polar opposites. If I am seeking your approval, then I am not in my knowing. In those situations of approval seeking, I am aligning to you instead of aligning to God/Source/Love/Energy.

The question is, what are you aligning yourself to—the status quo, your role, your class, your race or gender, being comfortable?

Take a moment to reflect and write your answers below: (Worksheet 3)

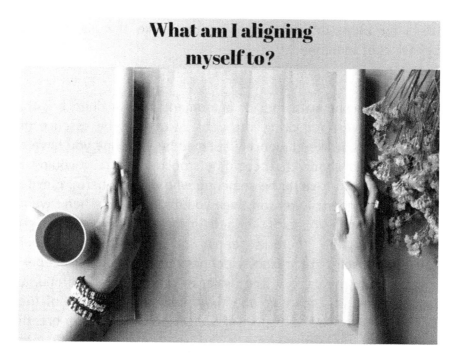

What am I aligning myself to?

We always have choices—to align with the frequency of Love, or to seek approval and recognition. We can make decisions from our Christ consciousness, or we can make decisions based on our ego, which is usually our persona. The time to release the false self is now. The time to embrace Truth and the knowing that each of us is an aspect of the Creator is now.

How do we start to consciously shift our focus and beliefs? The start begins from living our lives from the energy and frequency of Love. Love is being of and as the Universal Creator. Love is not a feeling, it is God in action, a frequency. Being the frequency of Love shifts us from believing in separation to knowing we are all of Oneness, even when it may not appear that way. By vibrating and being in resonance with Love to all, we meet, we affirm our Oneness.

To align to this new frequency is simply saying *I am resonating as Love in all I think, in all I say, and in all my actions.* This is really an easy practice when we are with people we like and understand. It's a bit more difficult when we don't like the actions and behaviors of someone.

Exercise: Imagine with me for a moment...take a deep breath, close your eyes, and bring into your awareness the essence of someone you dislike immensely. It could be someone you have a broken relationship with, it could be a political figure, it could be your parents, or it could be someone who did you harm. I invite you to remember the reasons why you dislike them. Then I want you to continue to hold this person in your mind as you go deeper...pass the rhetoric...deeper pass the dislike...deeper through the self-righteousness...deeper through the ego...deeper. Imagine that you can see the flicker of a bright spark of energy within them. This spark is who they really are, the light of the Divine, they too are an aspect of the Divine. Take a deep breath and blow softly into their spark and watch its intensity glow as you breathe. Take another deep breath and open your eyes. (Worksheet 4)

What feelings or thoughts came up for you as you completed this exercise?

Perhaps, you didn't like seeing them as an aspect of God...this would mean you might have to give up your righteous indignation. Perhaps you realized that they were acting from a place of fear. Perhaps you were able to see them as a child who endured tremendous trauma. The reality is we are all from God, from Light, from Love. Some people forget this Truth, and their actions and behaviors are so hateful it can be hard to remember this is their Truth as well. But our work as Truth workers— enlightened beings—is to first remember this universal Truth: *we*

are all an aspect of the Divine, and the second is to help people *remember this Truth* as well.

When we are on the receiving end of someone's inappropriate behavior, we do not have to make them evil, bad, or wrong, even when we vehemently disagree with them. We can choose to affirm their divinity, send them love, while honoring our truth. Loving someone and seeing our Oneness doesn't mean we ignore or accept behaviors that don't align with our truth. It simply means we bless them as we release them. No hatred or fear is needed.

This is an important concept to work with in our culture today. As we observe the political climate of our country, we don't have to hate our politicians; we can affirm the spark of divinity is with them as well. Even though we may not be able to witness their actions as Divine, we can still know we are moving toward Oneness, even when it doesn't look that way to our eyes. This is not a passive stance. While we affirm the Truth, we also take actions by voting, dialoguing, and through sacred activism to implement the change we wish to see in our world. Love and action are not mutually exclusive. Love is not passivity. Love is the action of God in the world. The time to be Love in the world is now.

Once we are able to get past the dislike and hatred, which is the distortion of Truth, and can embrace the Truth of who they really are, we are then able to live from this awakened consciousness, aka, being the frequency of Love. But as in all transformations of consciousness, it starts with each of us. Can you get past your own distortion of self? Can you go deeper...past your own feeling of self-dislike...deeper...past your own negative self-perceptions to see the truth of who you are? (Q2)

In one of my previous careers, I was an animal shelter director. I worked in New York City for the ASPCA. I got into this field because I loved animals. From the time I was a little kid, animals would follow me home, sometimes on their own accord, other times with a little coaxing from me. Wherever I went I connected with animals.

You cannot imagine the angst I endured when I realized how many thousands of unwanted animals came into the shelter and discovered there weren't enough homes for them all. The reality of not enough people to care for so many animals equates to many animals being destroyed. This is why it's so vital to neuter and spay them, because these sweet, loving, and unwanted animals had to be euthanized because we couldn't find anyone to care for them.

As the shelter director, I had to authorize each animal to be put down. Each morning I would walk through the kennels and decide whose time was up and would be destroyed that day. I would sign my name on each animal's card. I did this job for about five years, and my life was complete chaos.

During my employment I would work with rescue groups, ship animals to no-kill shelters for hopeful adoption, and work with volunteers to foster pups. I would take sick animals home to nurse them back to health so they could possibly get adopted, which oftentimes made my own animals sick. I also had this recurring dream that the euthanized animals were at the gates of heaven and would tell Saint Peter I was a murderer and to not let me in.

I finally left this job for my own survival. I was out of alignment with my awakening consciousness. I was in conflict with myself and filled with shame and fear. Still years later after leaving this job, I was filled with self-loathing over having to destroy so many precious animals, so I punished myself by living a very small and unhappy life. I felt I couldn't tell anyone what I did in the past. I feared they would condemn me as I was condemning myself.

Of course, this was simply my own projection of what I felt about myself. In order to shift this level of self-loathing, I had to go deeper with myself to find my own spark of divinity. It wasn't until I could forgive myself that I was able to start honoring my own "DNA." It was necessary to remember my truth that I am an aspect of God, that I am beloved. I am a **D**ivine **N**ecessary **A**gent of the Universe.

How often do you walk around with your own guilt and shame? Do you ever have the thought that if someone knew what you did that they wouldn't even have you in their life, so you can't even imagine God would want you? We walk around in the world hiding our shadows, our limitations, our errors. Truth: *everything* can be forgiven. As long as we believe we are the walking wounded, we will constantly look outside ourselves for someone to love and accept us because we can't love and accept ourselves. We cannot be the frequency of Love if we are the walking wounded, filled with shame, fear, and blame hoping someone could love us. Emanating energy as the walking wounded is in opposition to the vibration of the frequency of Love, of life.

We cannot do anything about the past or about the future. All we have is now. In this now moment, we get to choose if we are expressing as our highest form or not. In this now moment, we get to choose to love others and be the frequency of Love. In this now moment, we get to choose to heal our body, relationships, soul, and mind. All change happens now. As Eckhart Tolle teaches, *the power is in the now.*

This is why it is vital to remember and know your Truth: You are a Divine human being. It's important we forgive ourselves for not remembering this previously. You are beloved, God expressing as you. You must know your DNA. A Divine Necessary Agent must choose which manmade systems created from fear it needs to disconnect from to be able to hold its true nature, one of being in alignment with Source.

A Divine Necessary Agent allows herself to let go of people, places, and things that no longer serve her knowing as an aspect of the Universe there is more possibilities than she can imagine. Your ascension in consciousness is vital to transforming our planet. Your ascension in consciousness is the Second Coming; it's not about a savior coming to save you. The second coming is you...you ascending in consciousness. You saving yourself, and you saving the planet. My beloved, *change* is the awakening. Now is the time.

Chapter 3

Being Human

We are Divine and human. Divine because we are of God, spirit, holy, sacred, energy, consciousness—all packed into this human body. The key is realizing that we are experiencing and living in duality. This human body that has a nonstop thinking brain, faulty programming, hormones, ego, emotions, skin, blood, bones, muscles, etc. We are the light and the dark. We are the best humanity has to offer and the worst of humanity. Is it any wonder that we are confused at times, even to the point of attributing our own duality to God? There is no duality in God. All things are of God. Therefore, we are all things.

It comes down to our perception of people, things, events, issues. Do we label the things we like as good and the ones we don't like as wrong? How we label people, places, and things is how we respond to them. For example, if my belief says that to be of God, then I must behave a certain way. Then what happens when I'm unable to be a certain way? Does that mean I'm no longer worthy? Does it mean I am no longer of God? Of course not! But for many of us we behave as if someone or something becomes the label we give it; we then believe the story we make up about it as if it is true.

If I believe that lust, jealousy, anger, or any other perceived negative emotion I experience is not of God, the human tendency is to do one of two things. I am either going to attempt to make sure I don't feel those emotions, or if I do feel them I will force myself to separate from God. I will buy into the story that I am sinful. In the future, I'll also do everything in my power not to have experiences that could elicit those emotions, and if I do experience those emotions, then I will sublimate or project them onto others through blaming and shaming myself or someone else. Even though we understand that we are having a human experience, there is this drive to avoid things that we, in our humanity, have decided is not of God. In this action we become fractured human beings living schizophrenic lives.

Sometimes I wish someone had created a manual on how humans operate. It would alleviate so much suffering and anxiety from humankind. If we understood that so much of what we see in the world is simply what humans do, then we wouldn't need to be outraged or scandalized by certain things people do. We would simply say, "Of course that happened, they are just being human."

LET'S TALK ABOUT...*SEX*

There is a saying used in the New Thought Movement, "What we resist persists," which simply means that whatever we are in resistance to will manifest in intensity or greatness. So if we are in opposition to our sexuality, our sexuality becomes an albatross in our lives. The reality is that sexuality is part of the human condition. We are driven to connect with another in sexual intimacy. It's a biological drive driven by hormones in our body. Sex is not a sin or moral corruption.

We all know what sex is, but sex is the elephant in the room when we think about our humanity and spirituality. Many perceive sex as the opposite of spirituality. Sex is something we don't talk about in our spiritual communities or in religion, unless in damnation. In her article "Sex, Religion, and Guilt," Maddie Silver writes this about religion and sexuality, *"It's difficult to grow into a healthy sexual being when you are told by religious parents and/or church leader that 'God created sex to be something beautiful and pure but should only be enjoyed in a marriage'—and only between a man and a woman. And that you have to be a virgin, preferably having no sexual activity before marriage—no masturbation and definitely no homosexuality."* If our spiritual understanding about sex started off with this construct as the norm, is there any wonder why there is so much frustration, confusion, and guilt around sex and religion/spirituality?

In my teens I remember hearing stories of the awful things that could happen if one were to masturbate: you could go blind, become promiscuous, and even get hairy hands! What??!! Where do these stories come from and why do we use them torture ourselves and others? In the book *America's War on Sex, the Attack on Law, Lust, and Liberty* by Dr. Marty Klein, he writes,

> "Sexuality is religion's worst nightmare, because it offers the possibility of personal autonomy. Anyone can be sexual; rich or poor, old or young, tall or short, educated or not. Religion attempts to siege sex as its own domain, claiming a monopoly or morality which primarily is about limiting sexual expression (rather than ethical or rational decision-making.)"

This viewpoint regarding religion and sexuality is rather apt. The condemnation of sex is not about temptation, morality, or God; it's about self-determination.

When we have people/institutions that have rigid sexual mores, it creates a construct of being at war with our bodies. Societally this creates an evil overtone about sexual expression. "The devil made me do it!" is an apt response many devout religious practitioners use as they grapple with acting out inappropriately sexually. Much of our culture attempts to resist, abstain, or become celibate from sex.

Is there any wonder that there is such inappropriateness around sex? The scandals associated with Catholic priests are simply a manifestation of resistance to what is normal. Time and time again, through the denial of the body, denial of one's sexuality, it forces the individual to act out inappropriately. If there is shame about having sexual feelings, denying sexual feelings, when one is finally forced to deal with one's sexuality, it will manifest in ways that are damaging to the self and others.

If a person is not allowed to admit they are sexual, have sexual feelings, or be sexual, when they finally give into those feelings, it's going to be acted out in the darkness. It's human nature to want to hide things we deem as bad. When the body is driven to have that sexual need met, it will get it met in some secret way. Usually the need will be met with someone who can be forced to be quiet through manipulation, coercion, guilt, shame, blame, idolatry, or conditional love. Those who are vulnerable, who may be more open to someone's influences, are more than likely targets of repressed needs.

How often must we read about or hear about our idols falling from the pedestal, the pedestal we have placed them on, due to being in resistance to human experiences? Spiritual leaders falling from grace because they are having illicit sexual liaisons. Celebrities and politicians using their status and power inappropriately, while damaging the lives of others. Wouldn't it make more sense for us to embrace our humanity and our divinity? The problems occur when we deny the totality of who we are.

As Divine human beings, we cannot deny our sexuality...what we squelch and suppress will come out in another way. There is often a misconception that being sexual is the antithesis of being spiritual. We have a human drive to connect sexually with another, and to the degree that we resist or embrace that reality is the depths of our angst or joy. The more we deny we are sexual beings, the more we constrict and detach from our bodies. It's through our experiences of our bodies that we experience God. It's through our experiences of our bodies that we get to connect with God.

In her article "Embracing Sexual Incarnation," Julie Clausen writes,

> "We are naturally obsessed with sex because we yearn for these connections in order to experience who we really are, where we came from and what we are capable of being...It is when we deny our bodies and refuse to embrace our flesh that we become broken...For when we repress our nature as sexual beings, we cease to be our full selves. This does not mean we must all give into every sexual impulse or desire we have, but acknowledge that they are a vital and normal part of who we are."

Our business is not about regulating who has sex with whom. Our business is about knowing our truth: we are Divine human beings. It's in the acceptance and the acknowledgment that we are sexual beings that we are able to discern and respond as opposed to suppressing and reacting.

By embracing our sexuality, we move from shame to empowerment. In the acceptance of our sexual nature as being a normal part of our humanity, we no longer have to hide sex or sexually abuse those who are innocent. When we claim our sexuality, we are free to feel good and be satiated when we have sex with another consenting adult.

It's in denying our sexuality that perversion is given reign. Perverting our sexuality means we become liars, manipulators, abusers as we embrace our shadow self as our only recourse. If we believe we are sinners, in resistance to God, then we perpetrate crimes against ourselves and others in the pursuit of sexual gratification. But we know the truth: the shadow always comes to the light.

If there was no shame in our sexual identity, we would be free to love who we love. Whether straight, gay, bisexual, lesbian, queer, transgender, asexual, etc., the label would be unnecessary. We would simply love who we love and celebrate our union. News flash: God doesn't care who you have sex with as consenting adults. The next question that is usually presented to me after discussing this shift in consciousness about sexuality is about children or rape. Notice: I'm *not* including children or rape; these acts are manifested from the perversion of one's sexuality.

The second question is usually about polyamory. Surely, that has to be unacceptable. I don't think there is anything wrong with people who are consenting adults in polyamorous relationships. As long as everyone involved is in agreement with this type of sexual relationship, it's simply how they choose to express their sexuality. Once again, the individuals must be conscious, self-aware, consenting adults. This type of relationship cannot be gone into under coercion or manipulation. It must be something all involved are able to communicate effectively about the dynamics in this complicated relationship.

Moreover, I'm not advocating indiscriminate sex because that is a perversion of one's sexuality. I am suggesting that being an awakened consciousness means that even when examining one's own sexuality, you make choices from your wisdom and light. If the idea of polyamory bothers you, then I invite you to take a look at it and determine what bothers you about it. The reality is that what consenting self-aware adults do in their bedroom (when no one is being hurt) is not anyone else's business but their own.

I don't think we are in these bodies that can have such pleasure having sex and intimacy that we should deny it is a part of who we are. I don't think the Universe would design us this way. The spirit and body can coexist in harmony.

What do you think about sex? Is sex incompatible with your spirituality? If so, I invite you to explore your beliefs and decide if it is time to shift your perception around your sexuality. What if you embraced your sexuality as a Divine human being?

Take a moment to reflect on these questions and write your thoughts below: (Worksheet 5)

My beliefs about sex and God:

As a Divine human being, I recognize I am here to experience all things. I understand that if God is all things, then through my divinity I am all things. I am the saint and the sinner. I am the lover and the fighter. I am courageous and cowardly. I am enlightened and stupid. I am powerful and I am naive. I'm the virgin and the prostitute. I am generous and I am mean. I am able to embrace all these aspects of myself because they exist, whether I choose to recognize them or not. When I recognize them, then I have the ability to integrate those aspects and to become whole, no longer living in a disjointed fragile existence. Through integration, I become resilient and powerful. I move out of the glass house into a comfortable and sustainable home.

YOU'RE TOO...MUCH!?

I remember being accused of "being too sensitive" by others, and feeling devastated. My thoughts were of this nature, *How could they say that about me, don't they know how resilient I am? Can't they see all the psychological work I've done?* You see in my previous belief system, "being too sensitive" was a bad thing. It meant I was weak and cared too deeply without being strong. Of course, if I believed that was true, then I would believe others perceived me to be lacking. You see, at that time I was a fractured being; believing that I could only be good attributes, I denied my wholeness. During that time, I felt at war with the world, that no one understood me, no one cared, and no one could love me because I was unlovable. It's in the internalizing of these false labels that we truly damage ourselves. As we internalize this false self, we project onto the world our own fears and inadequacies.

In my process of awakening in consciousness, I came to understand that an aspect of me is a sensitive being. I then explore what is sensitivity, how did it feel, what are the positive aspects of sensitivity, what are the aspects that can trip me up?

Through this questioning process, I learned that I have empathic gifts, I am intuitive, I can sense energy, and I realized that it's easy for me to take on others' emotions as my own, therefore, I must be grounded and centered to prevent that confusion from occurring. Through this exploration, I've included sensitivity as a part of me; it's not bad, it's not good—it simply is. This is the process of integration, of us moving into wholeness.

I invite you to work with me through this exploration, without judgment. Let's work with another example: *anger.*

Questions: How do you label the emotion anger? Is it bad? Is it unladylike? Is it needed to be powerful? Is it something you pretend you never experience because you are spiritual? Is it disrespectful? Take a moment to reflect on these questions and jot your answers below: (Worksheet 6)

My beliefs about anger

Whatever your answers are, know it's acceptable to think the way you do. We have been conditioned from the time we could reason that anger is unacceptable. We may have been told by our parents that a good girl/boy isn't angry. We may have been told by our family that we would be punished if we behaved with anger. Our religious family may have suggested that a "good" Christian, Muslim, Buddhist, etc. doesn't get angry.

We may have been given severe consequences by our teachers if we said angry words or acted in anger. We may have also learned the opposite—the only way to get attention/love/contact is by being angry and acting out. We may have embraced being angry as a rebellion to our conditioning, or because of experiencing life's injustices.

The first awakening is to know that it is human nature to feel anger. Anger is an emotion we feel usually based on our thoughts or perceptions of an experience. It isn't bad or good; anger simply is. It's what we do with it that causes us suffering. Do we suppress our anger, claiming we are not angry, it's not our nature? Then surprise ourselves with an angry outburst that damages relationships with our venomous words, or worse, injure someone physically by our actions? How often have you seen in the media a violent crime that surprised and shocked everyone the person knew? Or have you even surprised yourself by the eruption of rage that spurts from you during a situation or event?

It's simple physics, Newton's Third Law of Motion states, *"For every action there is an equal and opposite reaction."* This means when we use force to suppress emotions, there will be an equal and opposite outburst of said emotion. If in your belief system being angry is not acceptable, even though anger exists within you, you may choose to deny its existence. That's a lot of energy placed in denying what is. We can only sustain that for so long before that anger is forced out. Usually, the anger that is finally released against the long-term applied force of suppression comes out in an explosion.

The next part of this exercise is to explore what is anger. How does it feel? What are the positive aspects of anger? What are the aspects of anger that can trip you up? Give yourself time to ponder these questions and write your thoughts below: (Worksheet 7)

My anger feels, looks, behaves like:

I learned that anger is normal, and that being angry doesn't mean God despises me or thinks I'm bad. I am loved unconditionally by the Universe. I learned anger is quickly dissipated once it's expressed, and it's expressed appropriately when I address it early. When I release my anger, I'm free to forgive, love, heal, and move on. Anger expressed stops me from making up stories, inventing intentions of others, manipulating support for my viewpoint. Anger can also motivate me for my highest good; it can allow me to claim my worth. What I have to be aware of is *not*

labeling my anger as negative or unacceptable, while allowing my anger to be expressed as necessary.

No, this is not a green light to go and tell off all the people you have resentments against. The most important corollary is that your anger is your responsibility, not someone else's. As I mentioned previously, our emotions are fueled by our thoughts and perceptions. As I've immersed myself in my own journey of self-awareness, it's become clear that most of the time when I get angry, it isn't about someone else, it's about my judgment of an incident. For example, for most my life I have been overweight. In the past, when someone called me fat or made jokes about my size, I would get so embarrassed and filled with shame that I would become angry at the person. Thoughts filled my mind, *How could they be so mean? Why did they want to shame me?*

But the reality is I am responsible for my thoughts and emotions, no one else. This meant I had to look at what meaning I made from their statement "You're fat!" The meaning I made of this statement is that there is something wrong with me; fat is bad; I'm unlovable; I'm unworthy; I'm a victim; I'm different; I'm not the norm. My feelings were filled with shame based on my perception and thoughts about being fat. Many of these thoughts and perceptions were my internalized critical parent.

With this realization, I'm then able to continue to deconstruct my psyche. The reality is I am fat. How does being fat serve me? I feel protected; I'm no longer a sex object; I can focus on my life's purpose, joyous existence; I can acknowledge that I have made a conscious choice to be this size; I am free to create and embrace my power. How does being fat not serve me? There is a limitation to my physical abilities; my life span may shorten; and in this culture I will be judged and labeled negatively.

The next stage in this process is to really understand being fat is one aspect of my reality and I do *not* have to be ashamed. I can embrace fat as just is, not bad, not good. What if part of my life's purpose is to define fat in a new way? Then I really don't have to get angry when someone calls me fat. Because I know that as a Divine human being I'm worthy, lovable, unique. Sure, I can be disappointed that a person chooses to focus on my size, but that's on them, and they get to miss out on connecting with my Light and consciousness. I am all things; fat is one of them...just is. I integrate that aspect within my wholeness. Now the power of the word fat is diminished; it doesn't define nor denigrate me.

That's just one scenario to demonstrate that each of us truly has the power over our emotions based on observing and then being willing to challenge our thoughts and perceptions. The way we view the world is simply a construct that has been created by others in which we say yes to make that construct a reality. What we learn from our family of origin, the way they define the world, isn't necessarily Truth. It is simply our family's comprehension of how to navigate in this particular family system and adhere to this family's worldview. As we start to interact with other families, we come to realize that each family is different. Depending on how severely we are indoctrinated by our family dictates our ability to transcend their worldview.

I remember the first time I started to realize families were different. I was probably around eight and my family moved from London, England, to New York, in the United States. Suddenly my understanding of how to operate in the world changed drastically. It was little things at first; words had different definitions. A fag no longer meant a cigarette but a negative term for someone who was gay. Gay no longer meant joyous but now identified someone's sexual identity. Aubergine now becomes an eggplant. Oregano is still oregano but pronounced completely different. Then the other external differences became so magnified that I became the cultural translator for my family. The difficulty arose when my family did not want me to embrace the American culture. This meant severe restrictions in my interactions with others from my family in order to uphold our European culture.

Imagine the duality of my childhood. I had one persona outside and another persona inside. The two worlds did not necessarily intertwine well for me. My family of origin believed the European way was far superior to the American lifestyle. They saw Americans as crass and classless. We were to hold ourselves above this "riffraff." Any friend was never good enough, and we were under strict orders that whatever happened inside our home was not to be told to anyone else. Of course, this situation became unbearable and clearly created an "us versus them" worldview. I totally embraced their world perceptions, believed what they believed, saw God the way they saw God, and came to believe that life was hard and people were out to harm us.

It wasn't until I committed to challenging my beliefs that I found freedom and peace of mind. We have the power to be cocreators of our planet. We do it every day as we hold our beliefs, thoughts, and perceptions about things. Then collectively those concepts come into form. For example, if we are holding disdain, disgust, resentment, or judgment against someone or something, we are feeding the fear and manifesting the very thing we are against. That's what being a cocreator does; whatever we hold in mind as truth is what we create. Whatever we put our energy into magnifies and grows.

FAILURE IS *NORMAL*

Part of the human condition is that we sometimes fail in our experiences. Everyone experiences failures. It's how we learn, grow, change, and evolve. None of that happens unless we fail.

But most of us have been conditioned to believe that if we fail at anything, we should be ashamed. Somehow in our failures we have let others down or not lived up to our potential or become losers. Yet, failure is required for us to become...

Failure is defined in the dictionary as: 1) Lack of success; 2) The omission of expected or required action. The first definition, lack of success, is probably the one we think of when we think of failure. Notice, it doesn't say *who* we are is unsuccessful. It simply says what we were trying to do was unsuccessful. But most of us have internalized that definition to infer that if we fail at anything, we have become a failure. We have been trained that if we succeed in a task we are rewarded, but if we fail at a task we are punished. It makes sense that we would come to the erroneous conclusion that failing is bad.

But failure is neither bad nor good. It is a simple word describing what occurred in one instance. The second definition of failure, the omission of expected or required action, is my favorite and the one I use when I fail at a task. I've had to challenge my belief system and retrain my thoughts to enable me to use this definition of failure.

Recently I applied for a job as a senior minister for a spiritual community. This community touted that they were progressive, ready for a visionary, and ready to move from navel-gazing to being the Light in their internal and external communities. I was sooo excited at the possibilities. Finally I'd be with people who want to shift their consciousness to the next tier of awakening. I was invited for a long weekend for interviews, gave talks and presentations, and got to know the staff and congregants. Well, I didn't get the job. That was not the expected outcome or action that I anticipated.

Does this mean I'm unworthy or a failure? No, it simply means I was not a good match for the community and the community definitely was not a good match for me. My ego felt bruised. My thoughts were: *How could the not pick me? Don't they know how fabulous I am? Maybe my talk and workshop weren't that good. Maybe I should have shown up less authentic, less bright, and less powerful.* My ego was feeling hurt, angry, and fearful. But when I went into my core and aligned with God/Allness, I knew this outcome was perfect for my growth.

You see, this particular community thought it had transcended unconscious biases and was ready for change. They were not. They were still in the deep process of grieving and anger with the previous female minister. The collective consciousness of this group decided they did not want a female minister again. They wanted a male minister. Wow! I didn't infer this or figure it out; I actually had most of the staff and numerous congregants tell me this to my face. This community also touted diversity, but they were 99 percent white and heterosexual. Who did they choose? They chose the only white candidate, who was male and gay, and that was the right choice for them because affirming sexual differences is usually the first outward shift in awareness in the evolution of consciousness for New Thought communities.

I would have been miserable if I had become the minister there. Their actions affirmed who they were, not their words. Did I fail to get the expected action from my efforts of interviewing? Yes! Am I a failure? No! Did I dodge a bullet? Absolutely! Yay for failure!!

> "There is no better or worse, inferior or superior. It's figuring out where you're meant to be and then getting there. This is true in every aspect of your life. If you fight to stay somewhere you don't belong, it will never be good and never get better."

You may think I got the above quote came from an amazing philosopher, nope. I got it from reading a paranormal fiction book *Jinxed* written by Donna Augustine. Yes, part of my own integration is honoring my quirks and secret pleasures. Paranormal fiction.

Let's take the concept of failure a little deeper. What if we create a new definition for the word failure? Charles Fillmore, cofounder of Unity, a New Thought church, had a gift for being a metaphysical practitioner. His gift was to look at concepts and redefine them from the viewpoint of spiritual consciousness. One of Fillmore's definitions for failure is: a stepping-stone to something else. What would your life have been like if that was the definition you were given for failure? For me, it's given me freedom to be in the Divine flow and acceptance of what the current reality is. When I fail, I think, *Oh, this is a stepping-stone for something else. Ooh, I wonder what exciting things are coming next.*

I now know that failure is not something to excise from my life. Failure isn't something that is bad that I have to get rid of. Failure is something that I need as I integrate an aspect within myself, understanding that this is part of my humanity. Everyone fails. Failure allows us to question ourselves and ask questions, such as: Could I have done it differently? Was there another way to approach it? Is there something for me to learn in this situation? Failure gives us the foundation on which we build upon.

Success requires failure. Sir Charles Dyson wanted to create a vacuum cleaner that would be revolutionary. Did you know that he created 5,127 prototypes that did not go to market? He made 5,127 models that did not function correctly. Dyson spent fifteen years of his life designing this new vacuum cleaner. Today he is a billionaire. Why? He learned something from each failure; he built on those failures and tried new approaches. He knew that success requires failure.

> "The wisdom in changing our belief around failure is profound. We move from fear-filled anxiety to being centered and calm in the face of issues. Failure is the way in which we create anew." –Rev. Sheree

AGE IS JUST A NUMBER

If you are alive, then you will get older and your body will not work the same way it did in your teens or twenties or thirties... Yet our culture seems to be obsessed with youth and vitality. Our society venerates youth, and older people are viewed as less valuable. Somehow we have bought into the belief that getting old is shameful and something to prevent at all costs. We spend our time fretting over aging because we believe aging means we will lose our looks, health, joy, status.

There are billion-dollar industries devoted to maintaining our youth, stopping aging, restoring our beauty. Even when there is nothing that needs restoring. I once read a story of a mother and daughter who were at the dermatologist's office for an appointment. As they waited there was a video advertising Botox that would keep playing over and over for patients to watch as they waited. After their appointment was complete, the daughter told the mother that she wanted Botox. The daughter was sixteen years old, and the mother was actually contemplating it. This story is not an aberration; there is now an industry built around "teen toxing." Of course, this is an industry that is thriving off of people's fears.

There is a belief that we only have so much potential and there is an expiration date. We dream of finding the Fountain of Youth, and even though there is a location in St. Augustine, Florida, that says it is the Fountain of Youth, there is no such place we can visit to reverse our aging. How youthful we feel is really a state of consciousness. If we believe we are old, then we are old. If we believe age is an arbitrary number that has nothing to do with our perception of self, then we are open to decide what is next. Regardless of our age, we can choose who we become, what we want to do, how to reinvent ourselves for our next stage in life, and how much joy we can have in our lives.

What is the story you tell yourself about aging? (Q3) Do you tell yourself that getting older is a burden, that you will become decrepit, unwanted, unloved, unworthy, and that your life is over? If you tell yourself these things, then as you age you will become those things; it is called manifestation. Manifesting brings things into concrete form through our beliefs. If you want a different outcome to aging, then it is up to you to create a new belief about getting older.

It means choosing to release the belief that as you age your life is over. It means going within to your wisdom consciousness and remembering the truth of who you are...a Divine human being! As you go within, align with your consciousness with Source, and get clear about what is yours to do, and then do. The connection to Source and remembering your Truth acts as a catalyst in your restoration. Through this syncing in, you become invigorated, expansive, and open to new possibilities you couldn't have thought of on your own. You become actualized and impassioned, no matter what your age.

"As we claim our purpose, we step into our calling renewed." –Rev. Sheree

HIGH ANXIETY

Something else that is normal for being a human is feeling anxious; it is part of the human condition. Many of us think that if we are anxious then something is wrong with us. I will invite you to look at reframing that idea. What if being anxious is simply an indicator of your body trying to tell you something? As I've been discussing throughout this book, humans have created many constructs about how to live, what's morality, what happiness looks like, when to eat, when to sleep, what is family, what is religion, even what is God. But as we evolve in consciousness, our bodies are usually the first to let us know something is out of alignment with who we truly are...Divine human.

Anxiousness is not a bad thing. The dictionary has two definitions for the word anxious: 1) Experiencing worry, unease, or nervousness, typically about an imminent event or something with an uncertain outcome. 2) Wanting something very much, typically with a feeling of unease. Anxiousness is felt whether we are worried, unsure, excited, or even filled with desire and happiness. Anxiousness becomes a problem when we create a false belief that feeling anxiety is bad or wrong.

Think of your favorite holiday... When you were a child, you may have felt anxiety, but the anxiety was because you were so excited about what was going to occur. Maybe there would be your favorite foods, family and friends visiting, or gift giving. This same holiday, experienced from your adult self, includes all your past experiences of holidays gone by and may still create a feeling of anxiety, but this time the feeling may be coming from a place of unease. Maybe you're concerned Uncle Bob and Aunt Shirley will drink too much and start to argue, or the meal you prepared won't turn out right, or your brother will say something offensive again, etc.

Notice that in both of these situations, whether we are in anticipation or dread, anxiety lives. In both these situations we are not in the present moment. In one situation we are looking ahead, and in the other we are living in the past while looking ahead. In either scenario, we are living with the ideology of the construct of that event...what it should be like or how it won't measure up to what it should be like. We are not in the moment with what is happening now.

One of the holidays I enjoyed was Thanksgiving. This created holiday was to celebrate the bounty of the Pilgrims with the help of the Native American people's support, at least that was what we were erroneously taught in school. But in our lives today, we invite family and friends together for an orgy of food and drink, while we celebrate all we are thankful for throughout the year. In my home I was filled with anxiety about cranberry sauce. What??! Yes, in my mind as teenager and young adult, cranberry sauce would make or break my Thanksgiving. You see, I was the only one in my family who ate cranberry sauce. If my mom bought it, then I was loved; if she did not buy the cranberry sauce, then my needs didn't matter to her, which meant I didn't matter to her.

You may say that's crazy, but how many times do we get so caught up in minutia that we are out of the present moment with those we love? Maybe your issue at Thanksgiving isn't cranberry sauce, but maybe it's having the special china, grandma's tablecloth, the right type of stuffing, etc. We obsess about these silly details because somehow in our mind we have associated these things as necessary to have the ideal constructed holiday and therefore we will be perceived as okay, loving, caring, successful, living the dream, etc.

But the reality is that none of these societal constructed concepts such as holidays, success, religion, family, career, justice, health care, government, race, sexual identity and on and on are the truth of who and what we are or why we are on this planet. We are here to have experiences to grow in our evolution of Divine human. In order to do so, we must embrace the present moment, become aware that only *now* is real. This moment is all there is. This moment you are safe. When we get caught up in our thoughts and memories, it hijacks us away from this present moment and that is when we feel anxious.

It's really easy to forget our purpose when we have left the present moment. When we feel anxious it is a reminder that we are out of the present moment and likely in resistance to what is happening now. Because when we are in acceptance we are in the now. Another clue to let you know you are feeling anxious is if you find yourself in resistance and defensive, you are out of the present moment awareness. To release the anxiety we need to shift back to present moment awareness.

Here are some tips on how to shift back to the present moment. (Table 1)

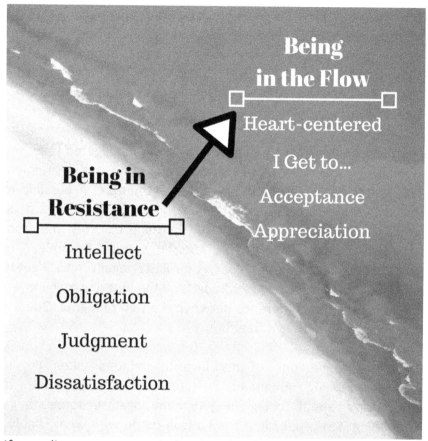

If you discover you are being bombarded by lots of thoughts, it means you have gone into your head where intellect reigns. The intellect does not create connection or intimacy in relationships. *Intellect creates a barrier.* To move from the intellect is to become heart-centered. All you need to do is move your focus from your head and focus instead on the area of your body that contains your heart space, and then put your awareness on your heart as you breathe into that energy. This creates a type of grounding, brings your awareness back into your body, which moves you from your thoughts to where you are in this moment.

Another way to be in resistance and out of present moment awareness is if you catch yourself having feelings of resentment.

Become aware of your thoughts, tune into what's going through your mind. Are you having negative thoughts about being with the people you are with at a given moment, such as through obligation? What is needed in this situation is to reframe your thinking about it being an obligation. Instead, find the gratitude of this moment and reframe into "I get to..."

Perhaps you are in a situation where you feel obligated to attend a family function and you really don't want to go. In this situation, it's easy to be in the grumbling of resentment. Is it possible to reframe this moment? Is there anything you can find to be grateful about the situation? If so, then you can turn this from "I'm so annoyed I have to go..." into "I get to..." Example: "I'm annoyed I have to go to my in-laws for Easter again" into "I get to say thank you to these folks who birthed the amazing man I love." Feel the energetic difference between the two thoughts. One is a road to hell, the other is freedom.

Let's not forget one of my favorite defaults when I'm in resistance—being judgmental. Here's what I've come to understand about being in judgment against someone or something: I'm usually in a comparison mode with what is going on, and I'm coming up lacking. Keep in mind that *being judgmental is an intellectual process, which means it's about separation, not connection.* We get so caught up in what we think things should be or should look like. We create unnecessary suffering when we "should" all over ourselves.

To move from a judgmental state of unconsciousness, I put my focus into acceptance of the person and/or whatever is the situation. This shift moves me back into conscious awareness of this present moment and my ability to be the frequency of Love. Example of judgment: "What the hell were they thinking when they voted for this person?" Acceptance: "It made perfect sense to them at the time to vote for this person, they made the best decision they could, and my job is to love them, their Divine humanity." Notice the energetic shift: resistance and anger moved into compassion.

Finally, we may know we are in resistance to the present moment when we are feeling dissatisfaction. Once again this is about where we are putting our energy and focus. Are we focusing on what's missing or not happening? If that is our focus, we will reside in feeling dissatisfied for most of our existence. To shift our consciousness into the flow of present moment awareness, we need to shift our focus to what *is* happening and what *is* for us in this situation.

Example: "I can't believe I didn't get that promotion!" shifting into "Not getting that promotion could free me for greater possibilities." When we are in dissatisfaction, we are in constriction, but when we are in a state of appreciation for what is and can see the good for us in the situation, we become expansive and in the flow of the Divine, while resonating as the frequency of Love. We become more open and able to allow good in our lives.

> "When you find the place you belong, it feels right, even on the worst day ever." – Donna Augustine (Jinxed)

WHO ARE THOSE PEOPLE?

Sometimes we make judgments about other people who aren't like us. Perhaps they behave differently, think differently, believe differently, or perceive the world differently. In those situations, it's sooo easy to think, *Who are those people?* Or what's more honest, *What's wrong with those people?*

As you know, life has a way of helping us to have experiences that shift us, grow us, and awaken us. Even at those times when we think we have evolved and are already awakened. As I've been sharing throughout this book, my own awakening was after I finally understood the truth of what I am. I am God manifesting. And I also understood you are God manifesting.

So imagine my surprise when I have the thought: *Who are those people?* followed by *What's wrong with those people?* For me, this is not a moment of shame, it's a moment of wonder and introspection. First, I realize I have a thought, and then I realize that thought is out of alignment with my belief, out of alignment with Truth. I do not freak out and flagellate myself for having the thoughts. I understand I am here to have all human experiences, so of course I can have all types of thoughts. The power is in what I do and how I react to the thoughts.

Any teacher of wisdom and spiritual growth must continuously do their own work of self-awareness to stay awake. This teacher must be unafraid to share all aspects of their humanity and divinity. For me this means I'm willing to be authentic, willing to share my foibles, my "aha" moments, and my "uh-ohs." God is in all things. No thing is not of God. Therefore I've come to realize that being of God means I am all things. I am the savior and I am the one to be saved. I am the alpha and the omega.

As humans we are all of the archetypes. Most of us want to be good people, but we often do so by hiding the aspects of ourselves we don't like. Hiding those aspects really means attempting to suppress them; this doesn't work. So those hidden aspects get projected onto the world as the things we dislike in others. Of course, it's really no surprise to me then that I have the thought: *Who are those people?* followed by my second thought, *What's wrong with those people?* But really, let's call it what it is; it's my thought about what's wrong with those people that is the issue. This mirrors my projection of the aspect of the self that is often focused on: what's wrong with me?

Now as a practitioner of Truth, I get to unravel where this thought comes from. That's part of what practical spirituality is about, being fearless in self-awareness. The thought comes from my observation of what's happening culturally in our country. One doesn't have to be a scholar to realize that the systems we as a society put in place to help us, serve us, and protect us aren't working the way they should in theory.

In our attempt to fix these broken systems, we vote and implement new laws that support these damaged systems. Then when they don't work, it's easy to say it is other folks who don't see things our way that are causing the issues. Albert Einstein has a famous quote: *"Problems cannot be solved with the same mind-set that created them."* Meaning we can't use broken logic to fix the damage caused by the initial faulty logic. It is only through our awakening that we create anew.

"An awakened consciousness creates anew." – Rev. Sheree

Today we live in a culture where people speak from their belief system as if it is truth. Human nature says, *What I believe must be true*. Often that belief isn't truth but a myth we have come to believe as truth. It can even be a belief in a man-made system that is perceived as truth, when it definitely is not truth. This creates dissonance.

The dictionary defines dissonance as a tension or clash resulting from the combination of two disharmonious or unsuitable elements. Dissonance is a lack of agreement such as the dissonance between the truth and what people want to believe; especially inconsistency between the beliefs one holds, or between one's actions and one's beliefs.

At the website Simply Psychology, in an article "Cognitive Dissonance," Saul McLeod, explains the origin of the term cognitive dissonance.

> "Cognitive dissonance was first investigated by Leon Festinger, arising out of a participant observation study of a cult which believed that the earth was going to be destroyed by a flood, and what happened to its members—particularly the really committed ones who had given up their homes and jobs to work for the cult—when the flood did not happen….While fringe members were more inclined to recognize that they had made fools of themselves and to 'put it down to experience,' committed members were more likely to re-interpret the evidence to show that they were right all along (the earth was not destroyed because of the faithfulness of the cult members.)"

An easy example of dissonance can be seen when we look at our family of origin. We often expect our family members to behave in certain ways, such as the maternal mom who bakes us cookies. But the reality is the mom may have never acted in that manner, but it is the archetype we imagine them to be. The dissonance comes from the mythology of what believe "good" mothering should be versus the reality of our experiences.

For most of us our mothers are our first relationship, first love. The one we see as giver of life and sustenance. The one who will cherish all we are and love us unconditionally. She will nurture us, care for us, and lift us to greatness. She is the wellspring from which we accomplish all that's good in the world. At least that is the mythology as we understand it. Where did we get the idea of perfect mothering? It's part of the unconscious collective. At the website *psychologistworld.com* one of the fathers of modern psychiatry, Carl Jung's theory of the collective unconscious is discussed.

> "Jung proposed that we are each born with a collective unconscious. This contains a set of shared memories and ideas, which we can all identify with, regardless of the culture that we were born into or the time period in which we live. We cannot communicate *through* the collective unconscious, but we recognize some of the same ideas innately, including archetypes...An archetype is the model image of a person or role."

The belief in the mother archetype of unconditional love, acceptance, and nurturing of her child is so ingrained in our unconscious that we force ourselves to believe that every mother possesses these qualities. The dissonance occurs when we experience our own mother or other mothers who don't act maternally. When we have the experience contrary to our belief, this creates cognitive dissonance within us.

What we are seeing in our culture right now has a lot to do with the out-picturing of dissonance. Cognitive dissonance can be defined as a psychological and emotional conflict resulting from holding incongruous beliefs and attitudes simultaneously. What we are feeling in our culture right now is cognitive dissonance.

We can see cognitive dissonance occurring in many debates in our society. Debates on sexual identity, immigration, homelessness, and poverty are all examples of cognitive dissonance. We have cultures made up of people who are followers of many of the world's most common religions. There are basic tenets that are the same throughout many of the dictated creeds. For most religions, there is some version of the Golden Rule that must be adhered to such as "do to others as you would have them do to you," "love your neighbor as yourself." But for some religious practitioners, they've decided to alter the Golden Rule so it only applies to those who fall into what they define as the accepted norms of their culture/tribe/society.

If we truly believed the Golden Rule, then we would love and treat every person as worthy. So if a couple fell in love and wanted to be married, we would celebrate them, no matter their sexual orientation. But time and again, we see "devout" Christians, Jews, and Muslims who not only won't acknowledge gay marriages but go to the extreme of condemning them. There are also many Christians who see any person of color as less than human or worth less.

Dissonance is having the belief of loving our brother as ourselves, while behaving with violence/hatred/apathy to another. Cognitive dissonance is created when we have thoughts affirming separation from each other. And cognitive dissonance is so uncomfortable, we use logic, myths, and false beliefs to convince ourselves we aren't in dissonance. We all have stories we tell ourselves to reduce our feelings of dissonance. There is a physical uncomfortability when we feel cognitive dissonance, so we will do anything to end that discomfort.

In the example, I have the thought: What's wrong with those people? Since I believe that each of us is God manifesting, then this thought creates dissonance within me. Overcoming cognitive dissonance can be achieved through cognitive behavior techniques or by using spiritual practices such as Unity's Five

Principles. The text in () is an example of my thoughts as I go through each technique or practice as I work through my dissonant thought. (Worksheet 8)

Eliminating Cognitive Dissonance

COGNITIVE BEHAVIOR TECHNIQUE	SPIRITUAL PRACTICE
• Trivializing the inconsistency *(If they just pulled up their bootstraps and worked hard, they wouldn't have problems)*	• There is only one Presence and one Power active as the Universe and as my life, God the Good. *(Perhaps God had an off day when this person was created?)*
• Adding a thought *(What would my life be if I walked in their shoes?)*	• Our essence is of God; therefore, we are inherently good. *(Their behavior doesn't reflect the Christ Consciousness. How can they be of God?)*
• Change in behavior *(Get to know people who aren't like you.)*	• We are cocreators with God, creating reality through thoughts held in mind. *(I don't want to cocreate anymore wrong people in my life.)*
• Change in thought *(There is nothing wrong with those people; they are of God.)*	• Through prayer and meditation, we align our heart-mind with God. *(Denial: there is nothing wrong with them. Affirmation: they are of God. Prayer: how can I see God within them? Meditation: They forgot the truth; they are a divine human being.)*
	• Through thoughts, words, and actions, we live the Truth we know. *(Knowing this Truth, I get to show up with compassion and empathy. I am then able to treat them as a being of God, as I remind them of their Truth.)*

We can change the world, and it always starts with ourselves. For a week I would like you to become mindful of any thoughts that occur that separates you from others. As the thoughts come, don't judge them. Remind yourself you are simply having a human experience, to experience all things. As you become aware of the thought, remind yourself you are exploring. Don't make the thought bad or good; keep it neutral, which allows for ease in the discovery. Love all of yourself as you remember you are an aspect of those which you separate from. Be fearless in your self-awareness, while you hold yourself accountable to the spiritual principles.

THE FIVE-LETTER WORD: DEATH

Being human means we know that our bodies will eventually die. Unless we are Elijah, Elisha, or Moses, we are not going to be lifted up into heaven by the angels. Even Jesus died. Yet, in our society we don't like to talk about death or the process of dying. We have become so separated from an aspect of the cycle of life.

I remember the first time I became aware that I would die; I was about ten years old. Each time I thought about my own death, I would have severe panic attacks. At that time the only way I could get myself out of the state of panic was to run into a wall; I didn't know anything about grounding techniques. My running into walls was my attempt at grounding, and it worked for lots of years until I found better techniques of grounding.

My grandmother told me stories about her early life experiences of death. Death was seen as a part of the cycle of life, especially during her parents' and grandparents' time, a celebration of the person. The body of the family member or friend who died was not hidden away at a funeral home. The body was dressed nicely and laid out in a coffin, displayed at the family's home. Then people would visit with food and drink.

They would have a celebration around the dead body. They would share their memories of the beloved person; they would laugh and remember fond times. There were even stories of the deceased person being taken to different homes to continue the celebration. Yes, there would also be tears of grief, but for the most part it was understood that this is normal process of being human.

However, in our lives today, death is feared. Death becomes separated and compartmentalized from the human experience. We don't talk about death, and when someone we know has a beloved die, we often don't know what to say or how to comfort them. Our confusion about how to cope with death comes from death being hidden. And for those of us who do talk about death, we use euphemisms, such as: passed on, transitioned, lost, gone on, moved on, crossed over, etc.

Death is a polarity. One of the definitions of polarity is the state of having two opposite or contradictory tendencies, opinions, or aspects. When we talk about death, it can seem contradictory to our understanding of our soul's spiritual eternity. There are many opinions about death, such as: 1) when the body dies nothing remains; 2) upon physical death, the soul will reincarnate into a new body; 3) the body was simply a vehicle used by our soul to navigate the Earth plane, the soul continues after death; 4) there is no soul; 5) there is no afterlife; 6) there is an afterlife with God. Is it any wonder that we don't want to talk about death?

This section of the book is an opportunity to examine what you were taught about death, what you believe about death, and if you are willing to change your belief, if the old belief no longer makes sense to you.

Where do we get our beliefs about death? Our family and friends try to explain death to us when we are young. We often learn about what happens to our soul and body upon death from religious communities. The teachings from Christian sects give us a formula for eternal life...don't sin, accept Jesus as your savior, and you will go to heaven; sin and you go to the fiery pits of hell. Many religious communities have a crime-and-punishment mentality.

I cannot tell you how many times in different Christian communities I heard the phrase: "The punishment for sin is death." The reference usually comes from the Bible, in particular, Romans 6:23 states, "For the wages of sin is death; but the gift of God is eternal life through Jesus Christ our Lord." I don't know about you, but I've done quite a bit of sinful stuff, so I wanted to put off dying for as long as possible. I figured if I had enough time at living, maybe I could repent and not go to hell. This concept of death is powerful.

The reality is that *everything we say or do on this planet is temporary*. Death is the reminder of our mortal existence. Death is a big motivator for religious communities, especially if you want to ensure you and your love one has a chance for eternal life. It's also a way for religions to control behaviors. When certain behaviors are defined as sinful and seen as evil, then we will attempt to not do those behaviors, especially if our soul's eternal existence is on the line.

We will also make sure that everyone else conforms to this way of thinking, "the right way" of thinking. Our society is filled with those who proselytize against the wages of sin. In their mind they are waging a battle against evil, all in the hopes of saving your soul from damnation. I used to be one of those people trying to save souls from the devil. That is until I did my own research, looked at the belief systems I was taught, and discerned truth.

Ready to have your mind blown? Sin and punishment are man-made concepts. Humans make definitions up as a way to explain a perception or their understanding of things. That alone is commendable, but the bigger issues come when we believe it's true. There is no heaven and there is no hell. These are concepts designed by early church fathers as a way of defining rewards for acceptable behavior and punishments for unacceptable beliefs. We are not here on this planet to suffer; we are here to live full lives. Any pain we experience is simply an aspect of what we experience in life. We choose whether to turn pain into suffering. Suffering comes from our attachments to illusions and to specific outcomes.

Shifting the belief about death as fearful to a natural progression of the circle of life allows us to become empowered. Have you internalized your beliefs about death, heaven, and hell to mean that in order to get to heaven and avoid hell living a "right" life one has to be pure and saintly? No one is pure and saintly. We may have aspects of purity and saintliness, but we have aspects of everything else too. Imagining ourselves as pure is a road to purgatory. It is unattainable and creates immense suffering, duplicity, guilt, shame, and blame. We are spiritual beings here to have a human experience and to learn; this means we experience all things, not only happiness and joy, but pain and sadness too. A fulfilling life is not measured by your wealth or by your happiness percentile.

Our goal isn't to have long lives, even though in our society today the focus is on a healthy body and longevity. Our true goal is to shift and evolve our consciousness while experiencing everything we need to evolve while on this planet. With this goal in mind, evolution of consciousness, we can choose to have these human experiences while vibrating as the frequency of Love, knowing this is God expressing through us. Each of us expressing is the way the

Universe gets to know itself. We are made of stardust; we are a part of everything and everyone. There is only Oneness.

In his book *Discover the Power Within You*, Eric Butterworth writes, *"The divinity of you is that of you that is eternal, ageless, deathless, whole and complete. It is that of you that is perfect even when you seem to be imperfect."* So often we deny the truth of what we are because of someone's rules or laws. Yet, if we really see what we are, divine, then we would embrace the Allness that we are. This Allness includes our humanity as well.

Chapter 4

Religion is Mansplaining – Spirituality is Being Of and With God

I AM are two of the most powerful words a self-differentiated individual can speak. *I am* is not new, many ascended teachers have used this claim of power. Jesus: *"I am the way and the truth and life."* Buddha: *"I am awake."* Prophet Muhammad (peace be upon him) *"I am but a servant, so call me Allah's servant and Messenger."* Krishna: *"I am the beginning, middle, and end of creation."*

> "Therefore, claiming our truth is a powerful statement. Whenever we say "I am," we are claiming our Divine Truth." – Rev. Sheree

Having a relationship with God/Love/Universe/Light, whatever name you choose for your higher power, is not about dogma, credo, rituals, punishment, consequences, heaven, hell, purgatory, limbo, or any belief system. Your relationship with God has been co-opted and corrupted by our patriarchal society. The physical man known as Jesus of Nazareth was born at a time of great upheaval for the Jewish people. We know that the lineage of Jesus through King David was about the fulfillment of prophecy; he was to become the messiah, the one who would free the Jewish people from the Romans. Of course, the leaders of that time had their own expectations of what the messiah would be like, how he would behave; and they felt the people needed a powerful warrior to overthrow Rome.

The Jesus of Nazareth that is depicted in the Ancient Near East is the antithesis of what the Jewish leaders were hoping for. He was a spiritual master teacher who came to be viewed as a rabble-rouser by his own people as well as the Romans. He did not conform to the systemic structures because he saw them for what they were, corrupt and exhibiting the abuse of power against our humanity and divinity. Jesus spoke for those who were marginalized, for those who were poor, for those who were seen as damned. He called people to awaken and evolve their conscious, to denounce the laws of the land that were unfair and not of truth, while choosing to embrace the law of Love and Oneness.

The earliest writings about Jesus occurred around thirty years after his death. Those texts were a compilation of the oral recitation of remembered events passed down through the generations for those who wanted to keep the knowledge of Jesus alive to be shared within their culture. But as humans have a tendency to do, especially those of a patriarchal society, we create rules, regulations, tenets, creeds around what a relationship with God should look like.

Since those leaders of the first century were Jewish men, they formed new sects in which they dictated how one should worship God and emulate the Christ consciousness. Even more dogmas and rules were created as the Christian religion was co-opted by the Roman Empire and became the religion of the State. This was the beginning of Roman Catholicism. This was also a way for the Roman leaders to control the masses. Any other religions besides the Christian church became prohibited upon pain of death. Christianity became the religion of conformity.

Be aware that this wasn't how the initial followers of Jesus practiced Christianity. The early followers were having mystical experiences of God; and later after Jesus's death, they were having transcendental experiences of Christ consciousness.

Women were many of the core followers of Jesus; they opened their homes and hearts in support, in fellowship, and worship in a new awakened state. For these early worshippers their experiences included trances, out-of-body awareness, Oneness with Spirit. The Book of Acts tells of trance experiences. The Apostle Paul's conversion was as the result of a mystical awakening. In the Gospel of John, the writer was constantly in a trance state as he wrote. These early Christians were having metaphysical experiences. It wasn't about a creed or how one should behave. It was about communion with God.

Communion with God is *not* about a religious belief system. Communion with God is about connecting and aligning and achieving Oneness with all that was, all that is, and all that will ever be. This is how we awaken our consciousness. How we view God is the experience we will have with God. If I see God as mean and punishing, then I've created in my awareness a mean and punishing God. If I see God as love and light, pure energy, then God becomes love and light, pure energy.

> "The eye, in which I see God, is the eye in which God sees me." –Rev. Paul Smith

We can have whatever type of relationship we choose to have with God, Jesus, Buddha, Muhammad (peace be upon him), Shiva, Universe, Love, Light; the name doesn't matter. We can have a friendship with God, or create a relationship in which we worship a deity. Our connection to God can be one of enmity, camaraderie, playfulness, or apathy. There are no rules of how we have a relationship with God. It is humanity that fabricates false rules of engaging with God. We can have a relationship with God, Jesus, Buddha, and Krishna all at the same time, being in awareness that they are all an aspect of the Divine. The energy of

God doesn't care about a name or label. God or an ascended teacher...all is of God.

Rev. Paul Smith has a five-step psychospiritual process to help you build a relationship with God. He calls it "Sitting with Jesus." I suggest you modify this process and call it "Sitting with God/Divinity/Love/Light/etc." The key is that whatever name you use for God is appropriate. (Worksheet 9)

Sitting with God:

1. Welcome the presence of Jesus/God/Divine Feminine/Guides. Thank you, _____ for being here with me. *(Think about what you do when folks visit: you make them feel welcomed, you are happy to see them and tell them, you offer food, drink, etc.)*

2. Connect heart to heart by crossing the devotional threshold. You must fall in love using transrational (beyond logic) devotion. *(Make this a heartfelt connection. This moves _____ from a historical figure or intellectual thought into a living presence. What would it feel like if _____ were here with me now?)*

3. Sit quietly in mutual awareness. *(Enjoy the now moment, enjoy the company of the beloved, soak up the love, be in the field of love)*

4. Communicate back and forth. *(Allow all your senses to be present, stay aware of incoming: words, pictures, feelings, physical touch)*

5. Resting as Infinite Being. *(Because once you become connected to the Divine, you can't help but know yourself as infinite too. This is about merging with the Divine.)*

Should you like to be guided in this process, below is link to a meditation I created for you to try: https://www.youtube.com/watch?v=2hxJGuvWRnA

I know that there is a higher power, by whatever name I choose to use. But I don't subscribe to a particular church doctrine. I allow my relationship with God to be fluid, to have its own rhythm, and I find peace in the unknown, in the undefinable.

NO DEGREE OF SEPARATION

Even though we often say we believe in loving our brothers and sisters as ourselves, we continue to perpetrate violence against those who are different, while claiming God's love. There are many wars going on in the world today based on people believing differently or having a differing ethnicity or because someone's skin color is different. It's seems that the idea of loving our neighbor as ourselves has become tribal, meaning it applies only if you are part of my posse. If you are part of my tribe, then it makes sense to respect you as I would like to be respected by you. But if you are not part of my tribe, you are deemed to be "other" and not worthy of the same.

A degree of separation is defined as a measure of social distance between people. You are one degree of separation from everyone you know, you are two degrees of separation from everyone they know, and so on. There has been a prevailing meme that we are six degrees of separation from everyone on the planet. If we are all an aspect of God, then it is quite plausible that each person on this planet is an aspect of each other. As an expression of God manifesting, then it doesn't matter if someone is Islamic, Buddhist, Christian, black, white, male, female, lesbian, gay, transgender, tall, short, skinny, fat, etc. None of those labels matter if we start thinking of each other in terms of no degree of separation. I am an aspect of the Divine; you are an aspect of the Divine. Therefore, you are worthy of being seen, being valued, being loved, being respected, being treated with kindness, being treated as if your existence matters.

This book's mission is to remind you the power to uncreate that which is no longer working in society is in your hands. Separation from each other is a created myth that is no longer working. Separation from each other is a concept that was created in fear to control the masses. Being a Divine Necessary Agent gives you the purpose and calling to dismantle systems that create separation.

I was privileged to listen to a keynote speech given by Father Boyle, a Jesuit priest who founded Home Boy Industries, which works with the gangs in Los Angeles. He is known for helping gang members who no longer want to be part of a gang to find a way to leave, while making financial strides toward independence. He told of a time in his past when he was asked, "Why are there gangs?" He explained there are lots of theories as to why there are gangs, but he summarized it simply by saying, *"There are gangs because gang members have a sense of hopelessness. They cannot see themselves in the future."*

When a gang member enters into working at Home Boy Industries, he then is usually working with someone from an opposing gang, someone he would have tried to kill if he were still in his gang. Instead, what happens as they work together is that they form kinship. Father Boyle says, *"Kinship is one of the highest aspects of spirituality."*

But what is kinship? The term kinship, as I understood it, meant people bound to each other by blood or marriage. But obviously, that's not the type of kinship Father Boyle is describing. *The Dictionary of Anthropology* describes kinship as: "kinship system includes socially recognized relationships based on supposed, as well as actual genealogical ties. These relationships are the result of social interaction and recognized by society." When we are in kinship with each other, we are connected, and we value each other.

In order to be living from the frequency of Love as a Divine Necessary Agent, we need to live as if we are in kinship with everyone we meet and know. The reality is as God expressing there is no degree of separation between us. No degree of separation means we would treat each other with kindness and acceptance; each of us is valued and wanted. This is about going beyond the ego, beyond the senses, beyond our duality. This is living as divinity in skin.

YOU CANNOT BE ALL THINGS TO ALL PEOPLE

Somewhere in our minds, we sometimes get the sense that if we don't meet someone's expectations, we have failed them and we are not good enough. But it is insane to believe that everyone should like us or should see our gifts. From the time we were children, we have been trained to spot the differences, and in spotting those differences we begin to self-differentiate and separate. It is part of the human psyche in evolving to adulthood. But often there are lots of growing pains in becoming an adult.

The need to belong is an emotional drive for us, while individuating is a drive to self-actualization. Our need to belong can be perceived as being in conflict with our individuating. The balance between the self and sacrificing of the self is often in a state of flux. If we put our worth in the hands of someone outside of ourselves, then we are prone to self-sacrifice our needs for someone else's needs. If we put our worth as the most important priority, we are prone to narcissism.

I remember sitting on a plane listening to the flight attendants give the safety instructions prior to takeoff. Usually, like the rest of us, I zone out from fully listening to the same instructions I've heard hundreds of times. But this time, I was fully present, and as I listened, I heard the attendant say, "Secure your own oxygen mask on first before you assist someone else." This got me wondering why they suggest such a thing. Wouldn't I want to ensure my loved one or child has their mask on first?

I discovered that should a plane flying over fourteen thousand feet high in the sky experience decompression in the airplane, there is very little oxygen that high in the air. The air is very thin at that level and above, and there isn't enough oxygen for us to breathe. Research suggests that without oxygen flowing in the masks, you would pass out in as quick as fifteen to twenty seconds. Without securing our own mask first, we would be unable to assist anyone else.

Our lives work similarly. We cannot be any good to ourselves or anyone else if we are unconscious, nor can we have the ability to show up and function healthily if we are unable to breathe. The term "conscious" has a few meanings: having one's mental faculties fully active, being fully aware of what one is doing, and the awareness of oneself and the awareness of one's own existence. Conscious is also defined from the psychological understanding as the part of the mind comprising psychic material of which the individual is aware.

We can take the analogy of the oxygen mask and apply it to our lives in multiple ways. We can first look at it from the literal level. In your life, are you flying around on anxiety or adrenaline? If you are busy, not getting enough rest, relaxation, you may be in jeopardy of running out of oxygen and being unconscious, meaning unaware. It's vital for us to be able to carve out time to breathe in our lives.

To breathe means to inhale and exhale freely; it also means to pause and rest before continuing, and to feel free of restraint. The feeling of expansiveness comes from giving ourselves the space to be, without doing. We need the space to connect with ourselves and with Source. This feeds us and inspires us to be all we are. There is the spiritual need to stop and know our Truth. From knowing our Truth, we are then able to access our knowledge of our Oneness with each other.

We cannot give, share, or connect with someone else if we don't even know how to connect with ourselves. Our self-care has to be a priority even when folks don't support us or don't think it's important. We probably have experienced relationships with people who can only see our value by what we do. They can be personal or business relationships. We can choose to buy into their BS aka belief system and keep doing until we are so crispy, we either fall apart or leave. Or we can choose to honor our own truths.

The term "unconscious" also has multiple definitions: without awareness or cognition, occurring below the level of conscious thought, not endowed with mental faculties. Unconscious also is the part of the mind containing the psychic material that is only rarely accessible to awareness but that has a pronounced influence on behavior.

Now let's look at the unconscious and conscious on a metaphysical level. In the analogy of the oxygen mask, we must put our own on first. This is meaningful metaphysically. In his book *The Kingdom Within*, John Sanford writes *"...if we come to the kingdom of God and act unconsciously, despising the things of the inner world, we can expect to be ruthlessly treated by the unconscious, for in our refusal to become conscious we have flouted the spiritual facts of creation."*

Being unconscious is not in alignment with our life purpose. Sanford is saying that by choosing to live our lives unconsciously, we will be held hostage to our shadow self. We will be captured by our fears, feelings of unworthiness, and living unfulfilling lives. *The kingdom of God is our spark of divinity within us.* Without going within, we forget our Truth and never remember our power and divinity to actualize our awakened self.

Being conscious is not always joy-filled. There is a misconception that being spiritually aware means we are always happy, healthy, and abundant. Being authentic means being an awakened consciousness and being willing to feel the entire spectrum because we know that whatever is in our awareness is for our growth. This means we don't label things as good or bad, or shy away from what are our next steps. Allow yourself to feel everything; there are possibilities galore. Sadness and discontent are simply Spirit's way of calling us up higher. If we are always happy, would we choose to transform or change? I know I probably wouldn't.

NO IS A DIVINE ANSWER

No one likes to be told no. As a species, we want what we want when we want it. We have the brain capacity to make any need sound logical and plausible. This ability is a gift and a curse. In our ability to reason, make sense, and justify our behaviors and beliefs, we can elevate or destroy. Once again, the choices are ours.

But we can sometimes get caught up in the perceived unfairness of life. I belonged to a religious organization that I loved and believed saved me during a time in my life when I felt lost. I took many actions to become a part of this tribe, which included offering my services for free. And yet no matter how many ways I attempted to be of service, to be claimed by them as one of their own, I was told no repeatedly.

I kept knocking at their door by creating programs and workshops. I spent thousands of dollars to get additional training in an area I knew they had a tremendous need to fill. I justified my behavior by telling myself that if I find the right key or gift they need, they will finally see what they are missing by not having me as a part of their team. And still the answer was no. I also decided to become a minister of a large "progressive" community, and this would be another way for me to still be a part of the organization. Of course, the answer I received from several communities was still no.

Finally, I had to sit with the no answers without trying to force a yes. I had to grieve my desire to be seen and utilized by this organization while dealing with their unconscious biases. Allowing the space and time to feel the rejection and confusion, clarity bloomed and wisdom was born. I finally understood, *no* is a Divine answer. Without all those noes, I would be living a very small life.

The Divine noes led me and my hubby to release our home in the Midwest, for my husband to become a remote worker, for me to give talks in various spiritual communities as necessary, all while living in a motor home and traveling the country. The Divine no has given me permission to write and start carving out a new path; even as I write, I'm still not sure what it looks like. The Divine no says you are here for greater things than you can possibly see at this one moment in time. The Divine no asks, *Do you trust that the Universe is for you?* If so, know that you can wait for the Divine yes! I wish you lots of Divine noes followed by your life purpose unfolding.

"Sometimes 'no' is simply realizing you belong somewhere else. Stop knocking on the door. Step into brilliance." –Rev. Sheree

Chapter 5

Living in the Question – It's Perfectly Acceptable to *Not* Know

How does living in the question come into play? Living in the question is about living in the possibility, the probability, and the mystery. It allows us to bring clarity and wonder and heightened awareness to our experiences. We can use many sacred texts to help guide us when we are in those moments of the unknown. I have used the Bible, New Testament, Bhagavad Gita, The Apocrypha, The Gospel of Thomas, The Gospel of Mary Magdalene, The Gospel of Judas, The Vedas, The Upanishads, Qur'an, *The Life of Buddha*, *Truth of a Hopi*, *Science and Health*, *Lessons in Truth*, *The Science of Mind*, and *The Revealing Word* just to name a few. God inspires us to contemplate the Universe in many languages and religions. All is sacred.

When we look at the Bible and New Testament, the sacred texts of Christianity, we realize that they have been literally interpreted by many. But I don't think a literal interpretation is what we should do when we read the Bible. We should treat the Bible as a sacred inspired text, man's interpretation of their understanding about God at the level of their awakened consciousness.

For example, in the Bible, prior to Jesus's arrival, many of the books had to do with the health and well-being of the tribe of Israel. This was a time in human development when the health of the tribe meant the survival of the individual. The topics were about how people should behave within the tribe, ownership of wealth and lineage of children, purity laws, laws for eating that would be the healthiest for them, etc. This was a time of domestication for our species.

Today we have laws that help us navigate ownership, lineage, food standards, etc. Therefore, to say we must adhere to a literal interpretation of the Bible doesn't make sense for us today. We have been fully domesticated and taught how to navigate the existing systems of our culture by society. These ancient texts were written, rewritten, transcribed, redacted, mistranslated, over thousands of years, and they were written in the parlance of that time of society. The writers of that time wrote in story format, prose, and parables—short stories as examples of Truth. For us to literally interpret colloquialisms of that ancient time as the unerring Word of God makes no sense.

Let's look at one example written about a parable that Jesus is said to have spoken. It's the parable about the rich man getting into the kingdom of heaven. The parable is found in the Gospels of Matthew, Mark, and Luke. Jesus is said to have stated these words, "It is easier for a camel to pass through the eye of a needle than for a rich man to enter into the kingdom of God." There has been much speculation about what this verse meant.

"Some claim there existed somewhere in Jerusalem's city wall a narrow gate known as the 'eye of the needle.' The explanation is that such a small gate made it impossible for a fully loaded camel to pass through it. The animal would have either to be fully unloaded or walk on its knees in order to traverse the opening. The major problem with the above explanation is that archaeologists and other scholars have never found evidence of such an opening used by camels or reference to a gate referred to as the eye of the needle. Several Bible commentators have noted the Aramaic word for camel is nearly identical to the word used for rope. Some believe that when the New Testament's original scrolls were translated into Greek an error in translation may have occurred. This would mean the text should read 'It is easier for a *rope* to pass through'... Additionally, it is stated the words 'eye of a needle' refers to the small opening of the tool used to sew clothes and other things together. Trying to pass rope through such a small opening would certainly prove difficult! A third possible and likely explanation is that Jesus was simply using a commonly used saying to underscore the spiritual situation of those who are rich." [1]

You can see from this one example how important it is to do one's due diligence when reading a sacred text instead of listening to someone else's literal interpretation. I'm not saying we discard this sacred text. I am saying we use these sacred texts in a different way. Usage of the Bible and the New Testament is to inspire us, through story help us to know we are not alone, to help us connect to God, and to bring comfort/guidance when we are in need. We do this through metaphysically interpreting the texts.

Let's look at another example in the New Testament of Jesus questioning his disciples about their understanding of who Jesus is supposed to be. From the New Testament in the Gospel of Mark 8:29-30, the author writes about this conversation: "He asked them, 'But who do you say that I am?' Peter answered him, 'You are the Messiah.' And he sternly ordered them not to tell anyone about him."

---

[1] http://www.biblestudy.org/question/camel-through-the-eye-of-a-needle.html

Literal interpretations of this verse suggest Jesus knew of his impending suffering and death, and was warning his disciples of what was to come. Another interpretation suggests the placement of this question directly after Jesus performs miracles proves, without a doubt, that Jesus is the savior and messiah sent by God to save the world. Moreover, he may be helping his apostles shift in consciousness from what they thought he would become, ruler of Rome, to what he was a spiritual savior who must suffer, die, and be resurrected. From those literal interpretations, it would appear Jesus is the Divine human sent by God to save our souls.

A metaphysical interpretation starts with realizing Jesus came to usher in a new awakening of consciousness. Reminding us all that we too are Divine human, and greater works than his miracles we shall do. Metaphysically, the term Jesus refers to the Divine perfection of man; and messiah means the visible manifestation of the Christ (also known as Divine consciousness). We can metaphysically interpret that the question and answer in these are about the perfection of the indwelling spirit within us. But why shouldn't we tell anyone about our perfection?

I think it's because our ego, created persona, needs the answer; it feels empowered and confident when it has the answers. In the Western culture, we are trained to develop our intellect so that we know the answers. This perception of knowing is really a false sense of who and what we are. It's a mask that keeps us separated from each other and from our Divine being. Because when the answer is found, we think that the issue is closed and finished. We then strut about thinking we have it all together, nothing more to work on here. The reality is when we think we have the answers we lose the ability to shift, grow, and change.

Who am I? Who do you say I am? is to question our beliefs and our understanding of how the world is. This state is uncomfortable but brings a richer life. Without the questions, we are firmly entrenched in our false self, in our ego.

It is in the question that we find our purpose, our truth, our soul. When we think we know the truth, the moment we believe or think we know it all, we have closed ourselves off to possibility, closed ourselves off to Allness, and closed ourselves off to blessings beyond our comprehension. The time of living in the question is a time of transition. During this time it's important for us to adopt an attitude of "fearless openness" to considering that "what comes to us, is for us," to embrace and to learn from everything. All things have the potential to teach us, especially conflict and failed experiences.

During the time of questioning, *bring your whole self to the experience*; we don't need to avoid or minimize our anxieties. We don't have to put on our superhero costumes and our masks of competency in front of each. Instead, we need to embrace whatever level of grief, confusion, or anxiety that we may be experiencing. Because these aspects are part of us and are necessary for wholeness. This is not about revealing our ignorance. It is about demonstrating our authenticity.

During the questioning period, the overriding feelings often get distilled into the ideology that many things around us are changing. I use the word "distilled" because change brings many of our fears to the surface. So we may be focused on a particular issue, thinking this is the challenge and if we solve this, then all is well. But as you and I know, it's never really about the challenge. As humans we are very clever at disguising things in situations to dilute what is at the core.

Whatever the situation that is currently presenting, we may give power to this person/place/ideology by our own thoughts, interpretations, and feelings as we experience another person's behaviors. Notice I'm talking about behaviors, not the person. I'm making this distinction because we know that each person is of God. Although, sometimes they may forget who and what they are. From our humanity, our personality, our ego, we tend to focus on the slights and sordid words.

It could be something as simple as someone not returning our greeting, maybe because they were preoccupied with their own internal drama. But we turn their nonresponse into them being rude, raised by wolves, arrogant, privileged, or even not valuing us. And the real issue has nothing to do with this person not saying hello; the core is we are feeling uncertain and perhaps overwhelmed with the changes taking place in our lives, but it's easier to focus and try to control minutia.

Of course, it is human nature to try to control and manage the conditions that surround us. We postpone rest until we have figured it all out, but the reality is in a season of transition, conditions will almost never be right for rest, if rest requires everything to be in order. We need to allow ourselves to take a rest by bringing our attention fully to the presence of the moment we are in; balance is important during this time. Cultivate not knowing. It is not ignorance to admit that you don't know what to do next, you don't know how to resolve a problem, or if a problem will resolve itself. When we admit that we don't know, we open ourselves to new learning and create an atmosphere where others can do the same.

Be aware of presenting situations that can trigger you during this time of unknowing. It can be something as small as, "Why wasn't I invited (or offered or given)? It's not fair!" Or something as big as hearing blame from others for the conditions in our life. But if we are unaware that our buttons may have been pushed in that moment, it's very easy to opt to be defensive and "duke it out" with them. But if we stay centered in Love, Truth, and Oneness, we get to make choices. Do we engage at that level of impulse reaction, or do we choose to operate differently? The awareness of change and how underlying fears may cause people to behave strangely became clear to me recently. It was during the time when my grandmother was in the process of dying.

Gran waited until her immediate family members, which included grandchildren, to arrive before she was ready to release from this plane of existence. I know in my heart my gran gave me an amazing gift by allowing me the privilege to walk beside her through this transition. I got to be the one to tell her she was dying, to help her find words to express her love, and to pray with her for a gentle passing on. As my gran was going through the process of dying, our family was connected, members easily made time for everyone to have personal connectivity with Gran, and we listened to each other.

However, the moment my grandmother died, there was an immediate fight for power and authority. Here is the presenting situation: A family member displayed behaviors such as rigidity, control, blame, and disregard. This person changed the funeral date, took over all the arrangements, excluded our side of the family from participating, etc. It became clear that I would not be included in my grandmother's funeral. I was heartbroken.

My husband and I were planning to leave the day after my grandmother died to drive back to Kansas City because we inherited a parrot, a very large sulfur-crested cockatoo from my gran. The funeral was to be held the following week, at which point I would return. After we canceled our return flights and rented a vehicle to be able to transport this large and aggressive parrot, we received a call from this family member telling us the plans were changed and the funeral was going to be in a couple of days. I also was told it was imperative that I attend because how would it look if I didn't show up to my own grandmother's funeral.

How do I consciously handle this situation? I thought of my professor Robert Brumet's spiritual counseling model. I adapted this model to help me through my feelings. First, I *breathe* and talk through the facts several times, not from a place of relishing the slights and sordid words, but from a place of getting clarity of what I am feeling. I listen to my internal dialogue and determine what meaning I am making of this. Next, I feel all the feelings that come up, such as shock, anger, hurt, and then fear. Notice, in this scenario, fear is a natural feeling when we are in the midst of change.

Change is defined as to become different; to become altered; to become transformed or converted. While the concept of change can be seen as positive, unconsciously, our persona (humanness) fears this change. It is the fear of the unknown, fear of what this change means to us, fear of how this change affects us. Our persona tends to be hypervigilant and perceives change as a possible threat or a death of what we have known as our own personal world.

The fear I was feeling in this situation was covering up the needs I had: to belong, to be included, and to know that I matter. *Finding out what my needs are is crucial to this process.* If you find yourself in interactions with people and the feeling of fear comes up, don't try to rid yourself of the feeling or refuse to feel it. *This is where the gold is, because anytime you feel fear it reminds you that there is a hidden need you have.* Once you uncover your needs, the healing can begin. As I continued to explore, I am reminded of memories and beliefs from the past within my family that make it clear as to why I have these fears.

This is where our highest consciousness and all that time spent in prayer and meditation comes into effect. This is where I'm reminded of the truth of what I am. The more times I touch the stillness and connect with my divinity, the easier it is for me to remember, know, and then honor my truth. If we choose to be awakened, then we know there are more options than our humanity could ever understand. *From that sense of Divine knowing, we can then choose to await the answer that will give us our best options for the highest and best outcome.*

While awaiting the answers to my dilemma, it gave me a moment to pause and look at this family member in a new way. In this present moment awareness, I could understand their choice to act from a place of control and exclusion. This awareness allowed me to have compassion for them, even as I was being excluded from being a part of the service or planning of my gran's funeral.

The healthy choice became apparent; it was for me to leave before my grandmother's funeral. The decision didn't come from a place of revenge or punishment, or a flight-or-fight response. The decision came from what would serve me, Graham (hubby), our two dogs, and the cockatoo (Coco). Keeping my promise to my gran about taking and caring for Coco meant that we would have to drive from Florida to Kansas City. We were at peace; we had said our goodbyes to gran during her hospital and hospice stay, in a loving and authentic way. I was free from the burden of guilt or shame. I was free from "what will people think."

I choose to tell you this journey because I'm sure many of you don't have the Brady Bunch for a family. So perhaps, from my example, you may be kind to yourself when interacting with your family, as well as having some tools to help you navigate situations. One of the principles of being a spiritual being is that we are cocreators. While I know this is true, I also know "stuff/life" happens, but it is how we respond instead of react and the choices we make to that "stuff" that is the mark of being awakened and being cocreators.

As things change in your life, it's so easy for your fears to show up in numerous situations. Therefore, I wanted to remind you, it is mostly never about the presenting situation. This situation I described was one of many situations that occurred when I went home. Yet, the underlying distilled issue with all these dramas playing out is change. As the ruling matriarch of our family died, this changed how we would operate going forward in our family dynamics; it brought up many of our individual and collective fears.

Fears such as: how we would fit into our family system without my grandmother, fears regarding what roles we want to take on as power shifts, fears regarding our importance to other members of our family. So when you are going through change in your family, job, work, friendships, this is a wonderful opportunity to look at your roles in your life and decide how you want to respond to the changes.

This is why it's important to hit the pause button when we get triggered. When we hit the pause button, it gives us a moment to recognize what is happening to our system and to get clarity. We can ask ourselves questions about what is happening to our body: did our stomach tighten or have a sinking feeling; did our temperature spike; did we grit our teeth; did we clench our fists? If any of these happen, then we can be aware that probably our own buttons are being pushed. The reason to pause is to align ourselves within first and secondly to do our own work in shifting consciousness.

Once we have paused, we breathe to start the alignment process to our highest self. *Taking the breath oxygenates our brain and stops the amygdala hijack.* When we have an emotional reaction that is extreme in comparison to the event, we are being hijacked. Breathing takes us out of the survival mode of fight, flight, or freeze. Breathing allows us to move from lizard brain, which is primitive and reactive, to higher intellectual responses as we access the prefrontal cortex. Breathing allows us to have present moment awareness.

Being in present moment awareness is where we find clarity. In present moment awareness, we can hear beyond the words. We are able to see the energy and intention. We are able to be objective. We are able to hear another's words and our thoughts without attachment. In present moment awareness is where we find our own ability for self-awareness. It's from self-awareness we are able to manage our emotions and our behaviors. Amazing outcomes come from putting our own needs on hold for a short moment to garner greater clarity, wisdom, and to step into our Divine nature.

Without hitting the pause button, we are on a train heading in the direction we don't want to go. You know this train's destination by many names but the most common destination is called "Trigger Town." We often arrive at this destination at family gatherings where we go into it with the highest intentions that quickly devolve into us being angry and screaming as if we lost our mind and then our soul.

I'll tell you a recent visit of mine to Trigger Town. I visited my mom in Florida in December 2015. While I was visiting, she told me she was going to have knee replacement surgery the following week. I was surprised because we had been talking for months about the possibilities, and she was adamant she wouldn't have knee surgery. I told her I couldn't come back for her surgery because of timing, flight costs, and preparing for my final Licensing & Ordination (L&Os) interviews. These final L&Os were crucial to my becoming an ordained reverend. I also wanted to manage her expectations that this wasn't a time I could support her should she choose to go ahead with the surgery in January.

Mom decided to go ahead with the surgery in January, and the surgery went well; she was in rehab and she hated it. A week after her surgery, I could tell she expected I would come to her aid. I explained repeatedly that her brother, her caretaker, could advocate for her. She started panicking and created enough drama that she landed back in the hospital. My mother told the hospital staff that she didn't know who anyone was, she could not remember any family members, and that people were trying to kill her. Each time family called, she yelled and hung up the phone.

I started advocating for her over the phone with the hospital. However, it was limiting because she had my grandmother (now deceased) as the only person that could be given medical information. Finally I realized I had to go to see her; it was one week before my final L&Os. On my arrival at the hospital, I found my very lucid and aware mother. I was shocked!! I looked at her and said, "Are you telling me you don't know who I am?" I realized it was all a con for me to get there.

In my utter frustration and disbelief, I was able to hit the pause button. I immediately walked away from her and breathed. I was angry and hurt. How could she pull this stunt, when she knew what was at stake for me? I explained to my uncle that she said she did this to teach him a lesson. He was not fazed in the least because I was now there to handle the situation. He didn't have to deal with her drama. He made excuses for her and informed me of what my role as a good daughter should be. I once again was able to hit the pause button. I found some time away from that conversation with him, and I breathed.

It is only from our present moment awareness we can witness someone's divinity. Once we are able to witness another's divinity, we are able to see what may be driving them to say or do what they are saying or doing. We can have compassion for them. We then have the wisdom to respond from our Christed self.

It took quite a bit of processing time for me to get to present moment awareness. When I finally got there, I was able to see that my mom was unable to control her circumstances, and it threw her into survival mode. In trying to survive, no one else's needs mattered to her but her own. She was so far into fear and panic that the alleviation of those feelings was all that mattered to her. From this awareness I was able to see her humanity and divinity. I was able to shift from her being abusive to me to her simply being human.

Once we are able to attain present awareness, we can then press the play button. We can now be in inquiry with whatever is the presenting situation. We can ask for clarification. We can share what we heard and what we feel. We now have the opportunity to walk our talk and be the powerful beings that we are.

In my example, I was able to talk to my mother with love and clear boundaries. I was able to ask her what was going on with her. I was able to be kind to her and leave knowing I had put processes in place for her to feel safe. I was able to tell her that I loved her but needed her honesty in the future if she wanted my continued support.

When life gives us these upside-down moments and the world suddenly doesn't make sense, we always have the power to hit the pause button. We can also use this technique when we need to make a decision for our highest outcome. Hit the pause button and stop.

> STOP: STOP what you are doing, TAKE a few deep breaths, OBSERVE your experience, and PROCEED from a new level of self-awareness.

From this place of consciousness, we can determine if the situation is even about us or really someone else's to deal with. If it is about us, we can check to see if our personal fears are becoming magnified and then choose what to do about them. I'm suggesting that we be compassionate with each other as we grow on this journey. Many of the situations we experience in life allow us to come up higher in consciousness so that we can rise above the fears and misunderstandings. We get to truly trust in our divinity, knowing the truth of what we are: Spirit-filled love.

I'm asking you to behold your divinity by being in the question. It's difficult to be in the *uncertainty* because it's uncomfortable. But with these new tools to utilize in your development, you get to stand in your authenticity and in your power as you welcome new changes.

Chapter 6

Only the Shadow Knows

"Beware of the yeast of the Pharisees, that is, their hypocrisy." Jesus is said to have spoken these words when he was speaking to the multitudes in Luke 12:1. I love using the New Testament, not from the concept that this is the Word of God, but from an understanding that it is written by first-century Jewish patriarchal writers as they shared their cultural beliefs and behaviors, then analyzing the possible meanings for those writers back in their time period and seeing if there is any application for us to use in the twenty-first century.

I've chosen this verse to demonstrate that humanity has always had a shadow aspect that it attempts to keep hidden behind a mask/role of some sort. In this verse we will be looking at the pharisaic mask. According to some scholars, the word Pharisees means "separated ones." During their time period, the Pharisees were the priests who performed all the rituals for cleansing and atonement for the Jewish people to keep them in God's grace.

The Pharisees kept to themselves to be able to obey very rigid purity laws. They were a prominent religious sect during the first century; they were influential and prided themselves on being righteous. The Pharisees loved money, conspicuousness, and titles. They were so biased in their application of the law that it became a burden for the Jewish people to adhere to or comply with these laws. The Pharisees lost sight of the spirit of the law. The word Pharisee can be metaphysically interpreted, as "lacking in understanding of the truth; hypocrites."

During the time of the Pharisees, they were admired for their knowledge of God and feared for the punishment—oops, I mean, justice they meted out to the Jewish people. The Pharisees probably enjoyed being admired by the community and looked to for leadership. Some of you may think, well, someone needed to know the rules and lead the community. And I agree with you, leadership roles are important to a community's functioning.

Yet if someone becomes so self-identified with the role they perform, like the roles of judges, police officers, teachers, doctors, ministers, etc., it's easy to remain unconscious to the real self. In essence they have become a false self. Just as the Pharisees looked good on the outside, by conforming to the letter of the laws, there were lots of shadow aspects hidden within them, because they lacked the understanding of wholeness.

Jesus knew the Pharisees were invested in their roles: the authorities of Jewish Law. In Matthew 23:25, 27, Jesus is said to state, "Woe to you, scribes and Pharisees, hypocrites! For you clean the outside of the cup and of the plate, but inside they are full of greed and self-indulgence. Woe to you, scribes and Pharisees, hypocrites! For you are like whitewashed tombs, which on the outside look beautiful, but inside they are full of the bones of the dead and of all kinds of filth." Isn't that a powerful description? This is literature.

When one reads those verses, it's easy to imagine how vile their insides were. "The yeast of the Pharisees"—the use of the word yeast in this descriptive phrasing is very interesting. We use yeast to change the property of something, such as dough or hops. The yeast permeates every cell of the base ingredient, molecularly changes the substance until it becomes something else. For example, if we add yeast to dough, it expands/raises the dough to become bread, or when added to the hops it ferments into beer.

Ponder and answer the following. Do the roles in your life define who you are? Do the roles help you to feel accomplished, successful, important, or give you a sense of belonging? Are these roles truly what you have come here, to this incarnation, to be? Do any of these roles engender feelings of shame, disappointment, or failure because you aren't living up to the expectations of others or yourself? Who are you, especially if you let go of your roles? Write your thoughts below in the lens as you see yourself: (Worksheet 10)

My Roles: What are they? How do I perceive myself by what I do?

We entered this world knowing our truth but may have forgotten due to our focus on the things we have been indoctrinated to do or become. The need for belonging, conformity, and being a part of our culture is very strong. It's tribal. This desire can lead us at times to live a double life.

John Sanford in his book *The Kingdom Within* describes the Pharisaic mask when he writes,

> "The mask is the person we pretend to be—the false outer personality which we turn to the world, but which is contradicted from within...conceals our real thoughts and feelings...used so habitually as a way to hide from others and ourselves that we become unaware we have assumed it...there arises a gulf between the appearance and the reality...a certain falseness has taken us over."

"Beware of the yeast of the Pharisees, that is, their hypocrisy." We've defined Pharisees and yeast, now let's look at the definition of the word hypocrisy. Hypocrisy is defined as a pretense of having a virtuous character, moral, or religious beliefs that one does not really possess, a pretense of having some desirable or publicly approved attitude.

The example of the Pharisees is one that depicts clearly the mask people wear with others versus who they really are. It also shows how people behaved in relation to their understanding of God. As we continue working on the topic of the shadow, I want you to keep in mind ways in which your masks keep you limited and separated from God. In what areas are you acting on the outside that is not the truth on the inside? (Q4)

I remember back in the day being on my own personal journey for becoming what I perceived as "Christ-like." In my unconscious way of thinking from my Christian framework, to become Christ-like looks like this: I wouldn't swear; I would love everyone; I would be completely peaceful; there would be no sex unless married, even then it would be devout sex; I wouldn't judge people; I wouldn't complain; I would always be happy; I would give all that I own to others. These expectations of me in the role of a Christian woman were unattainable. This meant when I couldn't live up to these expectations, I would feel like a sinner, a failure, and inherently bad. What would other people think of me if they really knew what I thought, felt, or did?

My saintly persona developed into a projection of my belief about what a "good Christian" should look like. Anything that I did that I felt wasn't "holy" would be hidden from others, and after doing that for a while I started to hide it unconsciously from myself. Yet I could see my defects in others so clearly. There would be judgments of others because of their behaviors, just as I internally judged myself. At that time in my life, I wasn't being or living from my Truth. I was living as I thought I should within my Christian worldview. I was also frequently exhausted because it took so much energy to keep this false mask in place. Inside I didn't feel spiritual or Christ-like. I felt I was a failure, unworthy, guilty, and filled with sin.

Our need to belong can increase our desire to want to be a part of and to matter to family and friends in our community/culture. And because of this need we detract from the truth of who we really are. We may divide our activities into public and private, visible and unseen, but there is no such division in the kingdom within. I remember as a teenager, my grandmother saying to me to use my "indoor" voice when speaking. This was to prove to others that she was doing a good job raising me to be cultured and well mannered. In that situation my gran perceived me as too loud. But I really wasn't, I was just joyous and exuberant. But in my gran's worldview, a cultured lady was never loud or crass. So I learned to use this proper, very appropriate, reserved mask with others.

Integration and wholeness come from us knowing and making peace with all aspects of the self. The parts of us that we think are wonderful as well as those things we have judged to be unworthy or not of *Good*. All parts of ourselves are needed to be whole, the light, and the shadow. The loud exuberant part of me is vital to my wholeness; it helps me to not take life so seriously. The sullen aspect of me is also vital to my wholeness: it is a calling from Spirit that I am in need of communing with Source. Our purpose is, to discover the kingdom is within us. How do we do that? We find the kingdom within by embracing all aspect of ourselves.

As we discussed earlier, a little yeast slowly permeates and transforms hops, so too will our hiding from our whole true-self permeate and create a false self. If we are committed to this false self, it is impossible to find the kingdom within. In the article "Evil Deeds, Essential Secrets of Psychotherapy: What is the 'Shadow'?" author Stephen A Diamond Ph.D. writes,

> "Bringing the shadow to consciousness," writes another of Jung's followers, Liliane Frey-Rohn (1967), "is a psychological problem of the highest moral significance. It demands that the individual hold himself accountable not only for what happens to him, but also for what he projects...Without the conscious inclusion of the shadow in daily life there cannot be a positive relationship to other people, or to the creative sources in the soul; there cannot be an individual relationship to the Divine."

In our culture the expectation of what spirituality should look like often forces us to have debilitating judgment about our shadow side. We do so at the expense of compassion for our self and others. We do this and pay a high price at the inability to heal our shadow self. There is a devaluation of the personal relative to the spiritual. But if God is the source of all, then God is also within our shadows.

Shadow is defined as partial darkness or obscurity within a part of space from which rays from a source of light are cut off by an interposed opaque body; the dark figure cast upon a surface by a body intercepting the rays from a source of light; imitation of something. From this definition we can surmise that a shadow simply stops the light from coming through. Our shadows hide the divinity that is already there within us, and what we project into the world is a poor imitation.

We need to be committed to uncovering the parts of ourselves we think are bad or not of goodness. Because those shadow aspects are there whether we like it or not. Our darkest feelings reside in our unconscious, and we try so hard to suppress them in the hopes that they will go away. But they don't go away; they remain in our unconscious. This means that who we really are will come to light, no matter how much we try to hide it. Because when we suppress something so long, it eventually comes out, and when it does it can be in the most inappropriate ways and inopportune times. In her Huffington Post article "6 Strategies for Integrating the Shadow," author Judith Rich Ph.D. explains what happens when we suppress our shadow sides.

> "Out of fear, we learn to override our darkness or operate over the top of it. Here's the problem with this strategy: Suppressing our shadow doesn't vanquish it, it only pushes it off the screen of our conscious awareness. It's like clicking the 'minimize' button on the computer where the active window gets shrunk and disappears out of

sight, where it sits in waiting until we activate it again. The same is true for our shadow. It doesn't go anywhere when we vanquish it to the nether regions of the unconscious. It simply gets put on 'hold,' awaiting a new opportunity to make its next appearance."

We read daily about people who suppress their shadow side into their unconscious and then have extreme meltdowns—the minister who is invested in his role as the holy minister but has the affair with the congregant, or the teacher who embodies the role of perfect teacher but molests a student. In both cases it could be surmised that they were denying and suppressing their normal sexuality of being human. In the situation where the leader seeks to destroy a gay person, he or she does so in the hopes of not dealing with their own homosexuality. Perhaps in this scenario they have embraced the false role of a God-fearing pillar of their community, therefore, it is impossible for them to be gay.

What of the mother who kills her child? Perhaps she may have come to believe that a mother is all she is and feels hopeless if she is failing in the expectations of her role. Or what of the student who goes on a killing rampage? Maybe he can no longer believe the role he plays and is unable to live up to the expectations of being an extraordinarily gifted student. You may think these are extreme cases, but how many times have you heard the familiar sound bite, "They were so normal. I trusted them, and they were such a helpful/good person." All hypocrisy will be unmasked. Integrating all aspects of who we are is integral to uncovering our true purpose.

The removal of the mask means looking at the shadow aspects of our self, the parts of us that have needed the letter of the law, as the Pharisees. Our work is about integration of all aspects to become whole. Once we embrace and love these shadow parts and shed light, we can then become self-aware and work from a higher level of consciousness. Removing the masks and facades is vital for us to enter the kingdom within.

I mentioned before the chronic fear I had as a young woman in my twenties. I used to have panic attacks about becoming a homeless bag lady in New York City, pushing the cart with my worldly belongings. This fear would keep my up many nights. I toiled in up to seventy-hour workweeks. I worked these long hours because of my desire to control this fear from manifesting. The mask I wore was of a competent, professional business woman who did whatever was necessary to be successful. Of course, by working all those hours for a prolonged period of time, I became ill and had to take a medical leave. On my return to work, I discovered that my mentor had written such a poor appraisal of my work that I would be rated below an acceptable level and targeted for layoff. You see, it was a numbers game to the company, and one of us had to be laid off, which required a below-standard appraisal.

Despite my mask of competence, I believed this fear of becoming a bag lady created the impetus for the possibility to come into manifestation. One could say that my fear and worry was a petri dish that supported the outcome of me losing my job. I think that even though I took action to create a prosperous life, my underlying belief system that I wouldn't be able to take care of myself became a self-fulfilling prophecy. Our inner states of consciousness become our outward manifestation of the world we live in. Author Judith Rich Ph.D. continues to elucidate the energy that can be unleashed from continuous suppression of our shadow self.

"But there's more to the story of the shadow, for while it is in the holding tank of the unconscious, it is gathering up a head of steam. Like a dog chained to a wall, the shadow will begin to strain against what binds it and seek freedom. Sometimes at all costs. Anything that is resisted or suppressed will be compelled to seek release. And when it succeeds, as it will, most often its expression is wildly distorted, having hurtled itself out from behind the force of our resistance."

Our country is in its process of doing its own shadow work. We are a country built on those who have and those who have not. Those who are told they are valued and those who have been told they are worthless. We live in a country whose story is the white race is the dominant narrative. Meaning the white race is the keeper of truth, while anyone else is suspect. The dominant narrative is white, heterosexual, successful, law-abiding, and supporters of the status quo. It's at the root of the very beginnings of our nation. We have made great strides to end racism, but we have a long way to go.

I bring this to your consciousness not to delve into race issues, which is not the platform of this book. There are a number of wonderful new books that shed light on institutional racism. *The New Jim Crow* by Michelle Alexander, and *Between Me and the World* by Ta-Nehisi Coates are courageous examples should you want to dig deeper into this issue.

The issues I'm bringing to your consciousness are the existing systems that dictate someone is valued while someone else is determined to have no value. Through our collective consciousness as a society, we have gone into agreement with these systems that label and then support certain people as valuable, while denigrating other people as discardable. Each time we are silent over injustice and strive for success in these systems, we say it is an acceptable way for our society to operate. In the past, we have addressed some of these issues to make amends, but the norm seems to be to make the injustices acceptable through laws and propaganda.

Today we are seeing a resurgence of hatred against those who are different from the dominant narrative in our country. For many, this is appalling. I often hear from people that say that they cannot believe this is happening in our time. The reality is that this hatred against those who are not the dominant narrative has been going on for a long time; it's had coats of paint that may have made it more palatable to those who are deemed valuable. But it's always been there. Diamond continues to shine light on the issues that manifest when we do not do our shadow work and allow ourselves to remain unconscious. Diamond writes the following,

> "The shadow is a primordial part of our human inheritance, which, try as we might, can never be eluded. The pervasive Freudian defense mechanism known as projection is how most people deny their shadow, unconsciously casting it onto others so as to avoid confronting it in oneself. Such projection of the shadow is engaged in not only by individuals but groups, cults, religions, and entire countries...in which the outsider, enemy or adversary is made a scapegoat, dehumanized, and demonized."

What's happening now is that this country's shadows have come into the light, ready to be healed. The hatred is now being seen by most of us, and we get to question this belief system. We get to ask, "Is this what we really are as a country?" and "Is this who I am and what I believe?" Asking these questions allows us to look at our shadows, heal them, and then integrate them, first individually, then collectively.

But don't ask yourself if you are a racist, because your ego more than likely needs to protect and defend you. Your ego will say, "No, of course I am not racist. It's not who I am." But the following questions are the types to ask because they allow you to start a nonthreatening internal dialogue about your beliefs, while determining if the beliefs are even yours or someone else's.

Do you feel you are more deserving than someone else? Do you think you have to get what's yours at the expense of someone else? Do you think your kids deserve a better education than someone else's kid? Do you think you should earn more money than someone who is an immigrant? Do you think working for an African American or Latin or Asian manager is acceptable? Do you call a woman darling or sweetheart? (Worksheet 11)

Take a moment to reflect on these questions and write your thoughts in the lens below:

Paul Selig wrote in *The Book of Mastery: The Mastery Trilogy: Book I*: "When you lift something to the light, you give it the opportunity to heal. When you cast something into the darkness, you actually give it power. So the intention to damn anything you see, to put it outside of God, is actually to empower it."

It's impossible to be raised in the Western world and not have biases; it's just the way we were taught in our education system. The issues occur when we continue to behave unconsciously, unaware that we do have biases and continue to damage ourselves and each other. We must do this work on an individual level first, then as more of us do the work, the collective consciousness of our society changes. It cannot help but change.

We are the sacred temples. There is no need to go searching outside of ourselves to try to figure it out. Once we shed light, the feared enemy within is no longer powerful. The integration and love of all that we are is who we have come here to be. I see who you truly are, both the light and the shadow. The light and the shadow are both holy. You are a Divine being. Your life purpose is to awaken to that truth. All aspects of you are Divine. This is how we start the transformation into something greater!!

Diamond confirms this truth when he describes in his powerful article "Evil Deeds, Essential Secrets of Psychotherapy: What is the 'Shadow'?" that the shadow self is also vital to our well-being by being integrated into our wholeness.

> "If it has been believed hitherto that the human shadow was the source of all evil, it can now be ascertained on closer investigation that the unconscious man, that is, his shadow, does not consist only of morally reprehensible tendencies, but also displays a number of good qualities, such as normal instincts, appropriate reactions, realistic insights, creative impulses, etc. Creativity can spring from the constructive expression or integration of the shadow, as can true spirituality. Authentic spirituality requires consciously accepting and relating properly to the shadow as opposed to repressing, projecting, acting out and remaining naively unconscious of its repudiated, denied, disavowed contents, a sort of precarious pseudospirituality."

WAR! WHAT IS IT GOOD FOR? ABSOLUTELY NOTHING!

It's interesting to see in this process of great transformation, things that no longer serve us are coming up to be released. One of those areas is the concept of war. There was a moment in our recent history that caused the people of the United States to quake in shock and fear. It's forever known as 9/11, when in 2001 two commercial planes crashed into the Twin Towers in New York City. Like many people, I remember where I was and what I was doing at the exact moment I heard about the planes going into the towers. I lived many years in NYC and the surrounding metropolitan boroughs. The World Trade Center was one of those places I hung out, met friends, had dates, and took visitors to the observation deck. My dad even worked there for many years before he retired. I considered WTC one of my haunts. The attack hit me hard, as it did so many Americans.

My immediate feelings were shock, and then I became angry. I wanted to blame those people who did this; I wanted revenge, and someone had to pay for this injustice. Our leaders at the time were also angry and wanted retribution. The president and political leaders of that time decided to go to war against terrorism. Most Americans were elated by this concept of vengeance against this heinous deed perpetrated against innocent civilians.

Almost 3,000 people died in the attack at WTC. The War on Terror has caused approximately 4,500 US soldiers death in Iraq and 1,454 Allied troops lost their lives. Over 246,000 civilian people died in Afghanistan and Iraq, many of them children. There have been over 50,000 soldiers and sailors wounded. The total cost of life thus far in this seventeen-year war is over a quarter of a million lives. This has also caused dislocation of people, approximately five million are either refugees or internally displaced.[2] This war was to stop terrorism, but do you feel any safer now? How can we? By our own actions we have fueled even more hatred and enmity with the Afghani and Iraqi people against America.

What we needed from our leaders at the time of the attacks on the WTC was to create a different plan other than war. Of course it is human nature to feel the anger and injustice of the attacks. But after the initial shock and anger, our leaders needed to breathe, sink into their wisdom, and access their Divine nature in helping to come up with new possibilities other than more death and hatred. It's in our ability to breathe and access wisdom that we can begin to question our beliefs. The leaders could have asked questions such as: "Was there anything that could have prevented 9/11? Who were these attackers and why were they so desperate that they felt their only recourse was to take innocent lives? What is the US foreign policy in the region?" Some pundits suggested that our economic and military support of Israel and the dictators in that region were contributing factors.

One of the greatest stories of Divine humanity happened during the 9/11 attacks happened in a town called Gander in Newfoundland. When the airspace in the US closed down and prevented other planes from landing, which was done in the hopes of preventing any further plane attacks, the planes had to be diverted quickly. Many of them found temporary landing in the small town of Gander.

As more and more people disembarked, there was a shortage of places to stay and eat. The people of the town opened their homes to strangers, where they fed them, housed them, and loved them. A huge connection and bond were created between

---

2

https://watson.brown.edu/costsofwar/files/cow/imce/papers/2018/Human%20Costs%2C%20Nov%208%202018%20CoW.pdf this community and the Americans who landed and found themselves stranded in a foreign land but loved as if they were family. Some Americans even created scholarships for the children of Gander as a thank-you for their kindness.

There were many acts of love on that day, stories of people helping others to escape the towers before they fell. People risking their own lives to save strangers they didn't know. Love truly won the day. Love is what transformed a heinous event into acknowledging the depths of humanity's ability to care for each other. The perception of 9/11 can be changed from a day of horror to a day in which Americans realized their Oneness with each other. The day can become the day in which the world realized their Oneness with all of humanity.

One can hope that we may have learned something from this experience. But the War on Terror continues. In our country today, there is still anger and blame being spouted at "those" people. Especially "those" people who are seeking asylum or refugee status as their countries are being destroyed by this continuous war and many other wars. People are struggling economically, and they want to blame someone for their struggle. Once again, it's human nature to have those feelings. The easiest targets for our blame and anger are toward those who look different and believe differently than we do.

Immigration has become a huge trigger point for many politicians and people who may feel their way of life is threatened. It's interesting propaganda that has created the myth that immigrants are taking away our jobs. Usually immigrants are taking the low-paying jobs that no one wants to do because the pay makes it impossible to take care of one's family. Sure, there are also well-educated immigrants who seek to come into our country, but that's always been the case.

The overarching issue isn't that immigrants are taking our jobs, it's that corporations, businesses, and our government have moved jobs from our country and outsourced employment to other countries for lower wages. These businesses have decided that they will have higher profits with cheaper labor costs. They don't care about your well-being or ability to feed your family. They don't care when they close factories and bankrupt towns.

The prevailing propaganda has fueled hatred within our country. Many people are now intolerant of those who are different from the dominant narrative. There are verbal and physical attacks against those of differing nationalities, sexual orientation, and speakers of other languages. But the good news is that as these intolerances and hatreds come to the surface it allows us to look at the hidden shadows of this country. The shadows of slavery, of unequal rights, of indentured servitude are steeped within our foundations. The shadows must come to the light to be able to be finally healed.

The answer is never war. The answer is love.

Chapter 7

Practice, Practice, Practice

Here's the deal. This book isn't magical. In order to really change your belief systems, it takes practice. Practice in questioning yourself. Practice in not making assumptions about yourself or others. Practice new ways of communicating and behaving. I know it sounds like too much work, but the benefits of *not* making assumptions and being committed to consciousness are significant.

When we are no longer living from unconsciousness and assumptions, we get to *Live in the present moment = Creating from the NOW*. This means really allowing you to become whole, powerful, manifester and creator. Imagine creating new relationships with family and friends that are steeped in Truth. How would you show up in the world if you could live your life's purpose as opposed to a facsimile thereof?

When we work the tools shown in these pages, we become a model for others. We show up as the living representative of love in action. This empowers other people to be their truth. When we are no longer in resistance to life, to what is, to whom people are, we literally change the vibration from conflict with others to love and acceptance. This commitment to practicing a new way of showing up in the world means you are making a way for your own spiritual evolution and prioritizing you as important–you matter. And guess what? When you treat yourself as a priority, so will others.

Let's be even more specific. Your way of communicating with yourself and others will completely change by following these simple reminders: (Table 2)

1. Ask questions: And get clarity, don't jump to conclusions, separate the facts from fiction. So here is the lesson–*ask more questions*! Don't get carried away in your own head about what is going on for the other person–*stop* and ask the question. Seek understanding in your relationships and conversations. I have to remind myself of this all the time, because assuming is a habit that we all form and it is a tough one to break. Assumptions are fast, easy, and they feel good because they are based on your own version of the truth. But the catch is, you aren't always right—sorry to disappoint you. Sure, sometimes our assumptions are bang-on but more often than not, they aren't.

2. Listen: Are you really listening to the person talking? Are you misinterpreting what they are saying? Are you finishing other's sentences? Sometimes we only hear and see what we want to hear and see. Take a moment to be present. Find that voice of yours and then respond with "I want to check out what I think you have said." Repeat that back to them.

3. Give yourself a break: This is life-changing work; therefore, give yourself a break. Be gentle with yourself. Sometimes we take three steps forward and then two back, but keep moving forward. Be comfortable in saying, "I don't know"—especially to stop making up stuff in your head.

4. Practice, practice, and practice.

SILENCING YOUR INNER CRITIC

Wouldn't it be wonderful if we practiced using all the tools and we no longer had to worry about negative self-talk? You may think by making the commitment to transform and implement new ways of being that any internal criticism would end. Experience suggests otherwise. Whenever there is an upheaval, transition, evolution, shift, or transformation in your life, the inner critic becomes very active. It's part of the process. This is normal.

In her article, "Your Critical Inner Voice: Are You Letting it Sabotage Your Relationships," Lisa Firestone writes about the importance of knowing your inner critic to enable you to stop unconscious destructive behaviors.

> "Identifying what our inner critic is telling us about ourselves and other people enables us to become conscious of the unconscious influences from our past. To break from our own destructive patterns, we must gain an understanding of the defenses we formed as children that once helped us deal with hardships but now hold a negative influence on our lives."

When I was a kid and teenager, my family would tell me often, "You have a lot of book smarts but no street smarts." After hearing it time and time again, I internalized that as my belief. This mantra came to mean to me that I was smart but gullible and naive with people. As a child I embraced my introversion because it was safer to read than to interact with others. I understand that my family was trying to protect me by challenging me to be savvy when dealing with folks. But I internalized "book smarts" to mean I was a victim waiting to happen.

As an adult my life reflected that belief. I had very few friends and was hypervigilant with everyone I met because I felt someone would try to take advantage of me. My facade was a sarcastic intellectual who would slice and dice you with words. The persona said, "You don't want to bother me or challenge me." Yet, inside I was so lonely and fearful and wanting to be loved.

If we are experiencing feelings, then we are having thoughts that are fabricating certain feelings. All we need to do is tune in to what we are thinking. Our thoughts make meaning of our experiences. Let's say, for example, we offered someone a beverage we made and they said no. Do we simply accept they aren't thirsty? If so, then our feelings would be neutral. Or do we interpret erroneously (more than likely) that they don't like the beverage, don't want to accept anything from us, think our house or food isn't up to their standards, they are rude, etc. If that is the situation, then our feelings become negatively energized with resentment or anger.

You always have power over the thoughts you have. If you choose to do this work. Doing this work means ending your suffering. It allows you to release things from the past that no longer serve you allowing you to live a full, purpose-filled life. This is about *shifting from fear to fabulous*. This will change your life.

First you must be able to know what inner voice you are hearing. When you tune within to listen to your thoughts, you must differentiate between your inner critic's voice and your wisdom's voice. Your inner critic is usually an internalized negative voice, while your wisdom voice is inspired from divinity. If you don't discern the difference, then more often than not you will be tuning into your inner critic's voice. A few distinctions between inner critic and wisdom: (Table 3)

Inner Critic Voice or Thoughts	Wisdom Voice or Thoughts
Blaming, Shaming, Guilt-ridden	Accepting, Loving
Mean or Sarcastic	Hopeful and Full of Possibilities
Constricting	Expansive
Punitive Parent	Individuated Self

It is important to know the difference between wisdom and critic. The inner critic voice is loud and overpowering because it's what we have internalized from our indoctrination to this world. Therefore, it's vital to know the difference. When you hear your inner critic, there are some steps you can take. Let's use this inner critic thought as an example: "My outfit looks hideous, and I look awful wearing it."

The first model was given to me by Dr. Jay Koch, a cognitive behavior therapist. Then second model is how I silence my inner critic. (Worksheet 12)

Silencing Inner Critic By Dr. Koch Cognitive Behavior Model	Silencing Inner Critic Rev. Sheree's Model
1. Is the thought rational—scientifically provable? (Answer: Not rational. I wore this outfit before and it looked lovely then.)	1. Pay attention and tune in to your thoughts. (Oh my god, this is such an ugly outfit. Oh, who makes things like this, etc.)
2. Feelings—does it make me feel the way I want to? (Answer: No. The thought is making me feel ugly; that's not how I want to feel.)	2. Name it. (Mine is called: The Punisher. Name yours.)
3. Goals—does it achieve any short- / long-term goals? (Answer: No. If I'm feeling ugly, I'm not empowered to want to achieve anything.)	3. Call it out. (What's going on? Where did this thought come from? Whose voice is this? Answer: Internalized parent. Why is this happening? Answer: I realize I'm afraid.)
4. Probable harm—is this going to cause me probable harm? (Answer: Possible. I won't want to show up to...)	4. Love it. (Do not try to suppress or excise the thoughts. It's about integration of the self to wholeness. Talk to the voice: "Thank you. I see you are trying to protect me. You did so in the past, but I don't need this any longer.")
5. Conflict—is it leading to internal or external conflict? (Answer: Yes. Then, it's your inner critic.)	5. Release it. (Free myself from that thought. Let it go.)

I've given you two models to appeal to left- or right-brain thinkers. Use whichever works. I'm suggesting you do this work to be clear that the thoughts or voice you listen to are from your highest self. The wisdom voice/thoughts are the ones that empower you, guide you, and direct you to your greatness. Know that often when we are in the midst of change, it feels uncomfortable, and that's the time when your inner critic's voice/thoughts get very loud. Be brave and know you can do it!

ACCEPTANCE

Hobson's choice has come to mean take it or leave it. It is derived from the story of Mr. Thomas Hobson (1545–1631) who hired out horses and gave his customers no choice as to which horse they could take. Hobson's choice is actually defined in the dictionary as an apparently free choice when there is no real alternative.

Thomas Hobson ran a thriving carrier and horse rental business in Cambridge, England, around the turn of the seventeenth century. Hobson rented out horses, mainly to Cambridge University students but refused to hire them out other than in the order he chose. The choice his customers were given was "this or none," quite literally, not their choice but Hobson's choice. According to the website *phrases.org.uk*,

> "[Hobson] He lived in Cambridge, and observing that the scholars rid [the horses] hard, his manner was to keep a large Stable of Horses [healthy]...when a man came for a Horse, he was led into the stable, where there was great Choice, but he obliged him to take the Horse which stood next to the Stable-Door; so that every Customer was alike well served according."

This can be a metaphor for life; often a situation presents itself in which you are supposed to make a choice. Yet the reality is only one choice is viable in this given situation. Acceptance means choosing the necessity while knowing you have done the best you could in the circumstance. *Acceptance then frees you to be open to additional future options instead of lamenting what was.*

Acceptance is a person's assent to the reality of a situation without attempting to change it or resist it. Resistance creates turbulence, fighting to change things; acceptance neutralizes irritants and performs alchemy to become empowered in the situation. How often do we say something isn't fair? We then resist what it is, sometimes to the point of self-destruction.

Yet those thoughts of bad/good persist as we handle adult life's situations. Not long ago, I realized I needed to have a meeting with the CEO of a company where I was interning. The only problem was that I didn't remember the appointment until I was in the shower; it also was the same time that the meeting should be starting. YIKES! Immediately I'm ready to call this situation *bad*. Let's look at what would have happened if I hopped on board the "bad" train.

I would have taken the express train to the following stops: remembering all the other times I forgot something, telling myself I'm getting too old to do new things, and the last stop would be affirming dementia is starting. Once I exited from the "bad train," my destination would be shame and judging myself for being so stupid for ruining my reputation with the CEO. I would have then changed to the local train that stopped at: convincing myself this mistake is who I really am, and probably would not have shown up for the staff meeting later that day. All of this would have occurred because I judged the situation as *bad*.

This time I asked myself, *Am I going to practice what I preach? Am I going to channel my inner wisdom and attend to my spiritual practice of acceptance of all?* This time, I chose acceptance. I accepted that I forgot, and made clear the distinction that I am not forgetful. I embraced my humanity and asked, *What am I to learn from this situation?* Acceptance of all, no matter what the situation is, is a teachable moment on the journey. If I'm no longer labeling things as good or bad, there is a freedom to accept whatever comes to me is for me. Reality—I forgot the appointment. Here's the other reality—I am human; this happens to human beings. This is not bad, nor does it make me bad or inept. The next question is, *What is this trying to teach me?* Answer: *Oh, I'm doing too much. There are a lot of balls I'm juggling, and one of them dropped. Oh, this is an opportunity to love myself and look at this situation in a new light, the light of "it just is."* Wow, *I'm still okay, still the Divine being I always have been, and I am not ashamed for being human.*

This practice of accepting *all* allows me to show up later at the staff meeting. I share in front of all staff members what happened, because there is no shame and no blame on my part. I take responsibility for my action; I apologize. And the world doesn't end, no one throws stones, everyone laughs with me (because at one time or another it has happened to most of them), and the CEO graciously accepts my apology. And I let it go. The problems arise when we call a situation, a person, a belief, an ideology as bad or good. I made an error; I am not an error. I forgot; I am not forgetful. In this example, forgetting is simply what human beings do when they are juggling many things. It is not bad unless we ascribe it as bad.

With this understanding in mind: I am free to be authentic, free to be love, free to be understanding of you, free to be expansive, free to be a nonanxious presence. This is why I call *acceptance of all* a spiritual practice. So many of us think we are either unique at one end of the spectrum, or abnormal at the other end of the spectrum. We think we are doing something inhuman in how we behave, react, think, or show up.

What would it be like if we were taught that making meaning and being anxious are normal for human beings? I think that our level of neurosis would be reduced significantly. Because so much of our anxiety is wrapped up in our fears of being different or of not being uniquely different or in being worthy or being too much or in having enough or not having sufficient. But if we knew that all humans have similar thoughts, fears, and anxieties, there could be a level of acceptance that this is just what being human is about.

Imagine the ease in any situation practicing thinking, "Oh, that's normal, just being human." No bad, no good. Imagine being forgetful and saying, "Oh, that's normal, just being human." Imagine turning our fears of being too short, too tall, too skinny, too fat, and saying "Oh, that's normal, I'm just being human." No bad, no good. It just is.

Our bodies are amazing machines and wonderful indicators of where we are in consciousness. The anxiety spike is our body's way of letting us know we have moved out of accepting all as a spiritual practice, have left the present moment, or labeled something as bad and unacceptable. That is the time to tune in to that judgment and use it as a teachable moment. Whatever the situation, how is this *for* me? (Q5)

The reality is there is nothing against me. Therefore, there is nothing that is not for me. To practice accepting all as a spiritual practice means embracing and integrating all of me—the overweight human aspects with the nonanxious presence and the joyous being that I am. A spiritual practice of acceptance is embracing whatever is happening as *for* me. A spiritual practice of acceptance is tuning into our reactions and taking the time to be with the reaction without judgment, knowing we are human, and allowing ourselves to work through it without labeling it bad.

I invite you to practice this spiritual path of accepting all. This practice allows us to move from being in a reactionary state of mind toward a responsive mind state. By accepting all as a spiritual practice allows us to move from reacting to experiences from unconscious, automatic, judgments, and actions to living from a place of awakened consciousness and responding to life with intentional words and action.

> "Acceptance is the most powerful thing in the world. Because when you accept something as it is, you open up to the possibility that there might be a better way trying to emerge. Acceptance allows you to look for the intelligence of the universe at work." –*You Are The One* by Kute Blackson

Acceptance also means having compassion for ourselves, knowing that we are continually changing, we are evolving. Some days it's with ease and grace, other times it's klutzy and chaotic. But throughout our process, we need to know we are simply doing our best at any given moment. Comprehending some days I will understand easily those things that used to flummox me, while other days I may not even remember how to open a door properly. Acceptance is knowing that in my day-to-day, I am doing the best I can.

To be in a consciousness of acceptance also means accepting ourselves. Each of us is a miracle. We are not here to be like anyone else, nor to develop gifts like someone else. We are here to manifest our own gifts, our own feats of greatness. We are not here to measure up to anyone else's expectations. We are here to measure up to our own expectations using the gifts and talents we own. So, if your greatest gift is a nurturer, then nurture to the best of your ability. If your greatest gift is to run, then be the best runner you can be. You are God expressing as you. Step into your gifts; stop trying to be someone else. Doing our best means we don't have to sacrifice; we have a right to live, love, and be happy. Doing our best means we are ready to meet any issues that arise, because we know whatever the issue is, it's for our highest good.

OUR EVOLUTION

How do we transcend the constructs of our family's worldview? Usually it begins when we start individuating. That's a psychological term that attempts to explain our process of becoming an adult and self-identifying as an individual, instead of an extension of our families. Individuation usually occurs in our teenage years in most homes. That's when we start rebelling against the status quo of our families. It's a tough time for all the members of the family system. But that time can become rougher if our family system is committed to the status remaining the same. For me individuation did not start until my midtwenties because individuation was not encouraged at any level. It was seen as a threat to the family system and was met with harsh consequences; for my family, the family system's survival was paramount.

For most of us, when we were young children, we trusted and needed our families; our survival depended on them. We trusted that we would have food when needed; we would have shelter, love, and a sense of belonging. We trusted that our well-being would be taken care of and that nothing bad would happen to us. However, the moment that trust was broken, our anxiety grew and we became fear-filled. Do you remember the first time your trust was broken by your family? It probably turned your world upside down.

Today, I have compassion for my family of origin. My parents were married too early because that's what was expected of them. My mother was so severely restricted in her childhood that she didn't have the ability to individuate, and the moment she had a smidgen of freedom, she became pregnant and gave birth to me at the age of twenty. Can you imagine how overwhelming that must have been, when she had only been on her own for less than a couple of years? I cannot imagine the fear and stress my parents were under. My dad continued to be the party boy; he was only twenty-three. My mom was forced to be the primary caregiver, and she thought her life was over.

Fortunately, their marriage didn't last; they were divorced by the time I turned nine years old. Notice, I said *fortunately* because they physically and verbally fought tooth and nail. Our home was a war zone. I remember being around eight and running from inside my home out into the middle of the street, screaming because I was so afraid they would kill us and each other. The violence was terrifying, and I never knew when it would erupt. As the oldest I also felt responsible for my brother. There were many violent events in our home, and many of those found me shoving my brother into the corner of our room and protecting him with my body. Talk about losing trust that I would be cared for and be safe.

My world became an emotional roller coaster. I looked outside of our family unit for love and care. Is it any wonder that I would be sexually molested? I was vulnerable and yearning to matter to someone. It's human nature to want to be loved and cared for. It drives us. Sometimes that drive encourages us to reach for the stars; other times we may dive into the depths of despair and deprivation. We cannot undo what harm was done to us as children, but we can make a decision to heal from the damage and become whole. It's not an easy process, but if we don't choose to heal we become stuck in a perpetual loop trying to right those wrongs.

As human beings it's in our nature to survive. We will adapt and subsume ourselves in order to live. That was certainly my situation as an early adult. In order to start individuating, I had to choose to get psychological help through therapy to give myself permission to become me. My family's constructs were so ingrained that I would have panic attacks if I did or thought things different to their ideology. Therapy was hard work but it helped me to individuate and to start questioning my beliefs. *If therapy is where you need to start to unlock your identity, do your research, find someone ethical that you can resonate with.*

We keep trying over and over unconsciously trying to redo or undo our childhood. You know each time we find ourselves in the same types of relationships (names and genders may be different) with people hurting us, devaluing us, unable to love us...all because we hope, this time, we can finally prove to our families we are worthy of love. It becomes a vicious cycle of unrequited love and acceptance.

The abuse we may have suffered as children, we keep recreating over and over in an attempt to win this time. But here's the thing—we can never win by attempting to fix our woundedness. One way out of this cycle is by understanding how family systems operate, truly understanding our family operates from what they learned in their family systems; therefore, they can only recreate what they know.

Knowing our family of origin foibles was not personal, though it feels it at the depth of our souls, is vital to being able to let go of resentments. My mother couldn't hug, be affectionate or kind to me because she never was taught how to in her family system. It wasn't her life experiences. She thought a strong woman didn't show vulnerability because her survival was at stake. This doesn't mean it was okay for her to treat me the way she did. It means I can have empathy for her and release my need to continually blame her for the pain and damaged she perpetrated on me. It means I can find a way to stop sabotaging myself so I can prove to her and the world she was not a good enough mother. It allows me to take responsibility for my development, evolution, and dreams. I then become accountable for my actions and my life.

Here's another thought around the issue of family dynamics. What if my mother was exactly the way she agreed to be for me? Reincarnation suggests that our soul, the essence of who we are never dies; we are reborn again and again living multiple lives. There is a spiritual theory about reincarnation that proposes we are working toward soul evolution, toward a greater way of understanding and growth through our life experiences. There are soul groups, also called soul clusters or soul families, to help facilitate and support us through these varied incarnations. These groups of souls are deeply interconnected and travel together through multiple lifetimes. The belief is the soul cluster has gone into agreement with each other about the types of roles they will provide during each incarnation. These soul groups are then brought together in each life as mother, father, uncle, cousin, BFF, husband, sibling, etc., often with instant connection or recognition.

With this understanding, it would imply I chose my parents to help me learn what I needed to grow into or to experience to gain wisdom as divinity expressing. This ideology was a game changer for me. Before this realization, I was stuck in blaming my parents for not being the parents I needed for me to thrive. I would compare them to all the other wonderful parents out there and be incensed by the injustice of my childhood.

I was resentful, miserable, and unhappy. I was so focused on what I didn't get, on what was missing, that I didn't look at what I did receive. This also translated to how I viewed the world around me. I was always focused on what wasn't happening, what injustice I was experiencing, on the slights in life. It wasn't until I was forced to look at and then embrace all the gifts I did get that I started becoming more balanced. This is the beginning of healing.

Finding the gifts, we experience and feeling the gratitude for all of them is part of becoming whole again. The question starts with what good things did you get in your childhood? The first time I was asked this question, at twenty-five years of age, I said, "Nothing!!" I was so angry with them and the world; I couldn't find one aspect as a gift. It did take me awhile to find one thing...they taught me to navigate the world with poise and class. After a while I was able to find so many things to be grateful to them for, and each thing I found shifted my self-perception. So if you are struggling coming to terms with gifts from your family, I'll help you get started by suggesting a few and you finish the list: (Worksheet 13)

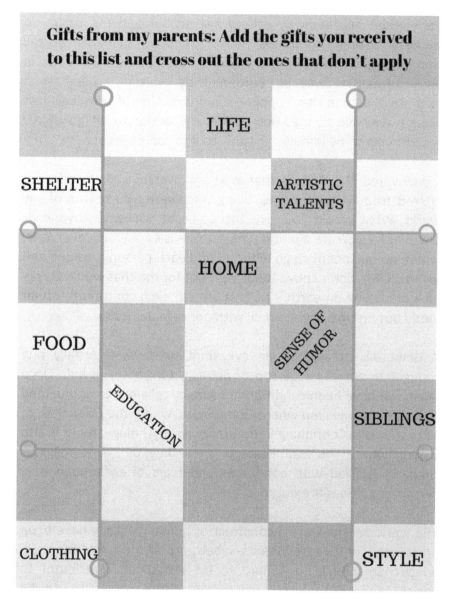

Gifts from my parents: Add the gifts you received to this list and cross out the ones that don't apply

LIFE

SHELTER

ARTISTIC TALENTS

HOME

FOOD

SENSE OF HUMOR

EDUCATION

SIBLINGS

CLOTHING

STYLE

It's in the awareness of all things, not just the things we perceive as bad or good, that we become whole. From my childhood experiences, even the ones I labeled bad/horrible, I gained gifts. After experiencing such a chaotic household, my desire for peace enables me to be an incredible mediator. My desire to be understood and seen by others has encouraged me to be an excellent listener to others, while accepting them as worthy simply because they are a child of God. Before this shift in consciousness, I was so burdened by walking around as a victimized woman that happiness and evolution of consciousness wasn't available to me. But only in my desire to let go of my resentment of my family was I able to find some success.

I discovered the Allness that is the Universe, and my life has shifted from victimhood to being a powerful cocreator of my world. What would you give to not be at war with anyone or anything? To create a world where there is enough for everyone, where no one needs to go without, and each person is valued and loved? (Q6) I don't know about you, but for me that would be my idea of heaven on earth. I believe we can each contribute to that world but first we have to deal with our own demons.

A demon is defined as an evil spirit or devil, especially one thought to possess a person or act as a tormentor in hell. Once again, we have been conditioned by many religions to understand that there is a heaven where God resides, where the Good Folk go after they die. Continuing in that religious mythology, there is also a hell, where the Bad Folk go after they die. This religious theology is filled with conditions and fears of consequences if certain conditions are not met.

The world religions are a construct of humanity. They have been created to contrive definitions, labels, moral code, and mores in which humanity is to adhere to be a valuable contributor to society. Religion became a way to control the masses, to use the authority of God as a means to have power and control over how people think and behave.

It makes sense for religions to create a heaven and hell as the eternal places to reward or punish individuals depending on one's behavior. Religion has conceptually created an ideology in which your soul, your eternal existence, is on the line based on your "faith" in the doctrines. Under this contrivance, religion has created a very powerful motivation for people to behave as religious leaders dictate.

Even more powerful is creating dogma that includes conversion or "saving another's soul" from damnation. What caring parent, friend, or family member doesn't want a member of their tribe to be safe? I don't know many. If they believe that your eternal soul is heading to damnation because of who you love or how you live your life or what you don't believe in, they will go to extreme measures in the hopes of saving your soul.

This doesn't make them wrong and you right, or vice versa. I know I'm stating an oversimplified understanding of many of the world religions' frameworks. Awakening to the understanding that the primary edicts of religion are to control behavior, you become able to choose your own evolutionary path, not based on dogma but based on your own inner wisdom. Religion is a construct, and each of us chooses to make that construct a reality or see it for the illusion it is.

The ability to understand our beliefs are simply manufactured by other humans whom we have gone into agreement with is one of the most powerful concepts in changing our thoughts and our perceptions. Understanding that many of our embedded beliefs are fabrications allows us to analyze and then embrace, new beliefs, which shifts our consciousness and enables us to cocreate the world we choose to inhabit.

I don't know about you, but for me, walking around fearing people, God, religious leaders, evangelicals, etc. will judge me bad for whatever I am or believe has been a nightmare. I am...some people will see my beauty and soul; some folks will only be able to see that I'm [place label here] and judge me as lacking. It's up to me to choose whether to put my self-worth in another's hands, or to celebrate my humanity. I am being human. This is where I am. I can fight it and not accept what I am, which I have done my whole life, or I can be at peace with what is.

One area that I find myself evolving in consciousness around is my body's weight. I don't remember a year that I haven't been on a diet and trying to lose weight. Guess what? I'm still overweight. I have shamed and blamed myself for being what I am, and been unhappy and miserable. What if this incarnation for me is to be an overweight Divine person? That frees me to accept my being overweight and celebrate that it too is of God. It also frees me to be joy filled, frees me to love me, frees me to be open and love you, and frees me to be the amazing Divine being I am, instead of trying to be other than I am.

Shifting our consciousness is a change in how we experience our essence/divinity/true self as we reside in these bodies. The questions are: who cares and why does shifting our consciousness end *isms* and injustice? The answer is: when we change, those around us are called to change as well. We create global transformation by the ripple effect we create by our own individual transformation. This is why doing our own work is so crucial.

It's clear that individual transformation is *not* about adhering to religious dogma, political agendas, control, fear, ego, or personality. Individual transformation is about saying yes to our life purpose and to the essence of our true self. Who we are is beyond the physical, beyond what we see, hear, taste, touch, and smell. Our energetic essence is more powerful than we can imagine.

Think of the phrase "the domino effect." It is produced when one event sets off a chain of similar events. It can be referred to as a chain reaction in which it releases a larger amount of energy when compared to the individual event or person. Buying someone a cup of coffee or putting money in someone else's car meter aren't large things, but it's an energetic shift in our worldview. Movements in consciousness happen from a tiny spark. We are often shown representations of the domino effect in the news when they show protestors or violence, such as the G8 or Ferguson Riots. But the same effect happens when kindness is given.

Aligning our frequency to the Christ vibration is *not* a secret or a new concept. Enlightened masters, teachers, and students have been doing this for centuries. Many of the enlightened teachers have been critical to raising humanity's consciousness. These lightning rods changed history. Yet there are so few of us willing to step into our truth, into our grandness. What stops us from doing so? Perhaps our fears. Fear of being alone or misunderstood. Fear of being perceived as crazy. Fear of being hurt. Fear of losing our lives. Fear of not being enough.

We have become so misidentified with our physical bodies that we fear the end of the physical, as if that's all we are. We forget we are eternal. Our consciousness is more than what's held within our bodies. Your Divine self knows no fear, hatred, or anger. It naturally vibrates at a higher frequency where it understands this world is temporary and is only here for our growth. Our spirit knows, even in physical death, nothing really dies, it's only transformed.

The question is: Are you willing to release false beliefs to become whole and evolve?

Chapter 8

Being the Frequency of Love

If you said you are willing to release false beliefs to become whole and evolve, then continue reading. If you said no, you cannot release blaming others for how sucky your life is, then I invite you to continue to read anyway because you can get a glimpse of how different your life could be.

The only way I know to find salvation is by becoming our own savior. That may sound blasphemous to some of you with ingrained theology that states that only through Jesus as our savior can we be saved. Metaphysically, I'm saying the same thing. When Jesus said in John 14:16, "The only way to the Father is through me." He wasn't talking about Christology; Christology didn't exist. He was simply saying being the frequency of Love and the awakening of consciousness is how we remember we are divinity. The only way for us to be saved is by knowing we too are the beloved, of God, and cocreators of life.

Jesus is a master teacher and ascended being, just as Buddha, Muhammad (pbuh), Brahma, Gaia, and many others. These teachers incarnate throughout our lifetimes to guide our collective consciousness into awakening at a higher frequency by reminding us of our own divinity. Each comes to help us awaken to Truth. It's part of the human evolution. It's hard to awaken to Truth when we are living lives in fear and control.

In the case of Jesus, he came onto this plane of existence during a time of tribalism and repression. In the time period known as the Ancient Near East; the rule of the land was to comply and adhere to the dictates of your tribe or die. It was a time of brutality and severe consequences for errors. Jesus came to usher in a new way of understanding God, the world around us, each other, and ourselves.

People, spiritual leaders, and rulers were asked by Jesus during that time period to challenge the accepted norms and rules of the society. He asked them, and therefore each of us, to question who are our brothers and sisters, how do we treat each other, who is deserving of love, do the existing religious dictates make sense, what does love mean, does adhering to the rules of the land mean justice or injustice. He taught us in parables, little stories that would make sense to the people of that time, to illustrate moral or spiritual lessons. Of course, as scribes and scholars tried to capture the essence of Jesus's teachings there have been errors, confusion, misquotes. It can be hard for faithful disciples to believe that a sacred text can be wrong; often what is forgotten is that men wrote these texts, translated these texts, and made mistakes as they worked on these texts.

The irony is that even as Jesus was all about questioning the status quo of his culture, his later followers have found a way to turn Jesus's philosophy into rules and regulations as they formed a new religion: Christianity. You see it's human nature to want a belief system that is perceived as unerring truth. It provides comfort and predictability. As a species, we abhor change, and yet as a species, change is necessary for our highest good. What if Jesus didn't come to start a new religion? What if Jesus came to help us shake off the ropes of bondage and discover our wisdom and light? Then we would be free to question our beliefs and to become the frequency of Love.

Frequency is defined as the rate at which a vibration occurs that constitutes a wave, such as in sound waves, or radio waves. Think of a radio station, when we are tuned into our favorite station— NPR, folk, country western, news, classical, metal, rock, rhythm and blues—what do we hear? We hear only the types of music that are played at that frequency. In our lives, whatever we are tuned into, that is all we are able to see, hear, and know.

In this analogy, the act of selecting a radio station is tuning in to the frequency of that genre. Let's say we tune into a rock station. As we listen, we are only hearing rock music. When we start grooving to the music, we come into resonance with rock music. At the point of resonance, we are vibrating at the frequency of rock music. Vibration can be defined as a person's emotional state or the atmosphere of a place, as communicated to and felt by others. Our body, mind, and emotions are vibrating as rock music.

Ever drive your car and feel drawn to look at the driver of the car next to you? When you look over, you see a person who is vibrating with their song. How do you know they are vibrating? Their whole body has become the song; they are nodding their head, maybe beating on the steering wheel, singing at the top of their lungs. In that moment they don't care who is around them or what people think. They are simply in the moment of being the vibration of that song.

Becoming the frequency of Love is about changing the frequency we may have been tuned into before. Maybe in your life today, you are currently tuned into the frequency of lack. In this scenario it would mean you can only see lack, not enough, or injustice because you are tuned into lack frequency. But now you are aware you have the ability to shift your frequency. We are discussing creating a shift from the intellectual understanding of transformation to the integration of being transformed. This means taking action, changing our focus and vibration.

To start this process, we first must get into alignment with the Universe. This is a simple matter of allowing our focus to be on our breath; our breath reminds us that there is something higher than our intellect or physical body that knows how to sustain us.

Focusing on our breath helps us to sync with attunement into our higher consciousness. As we become attuned, it means we are grooving to the frequency of God. We then start to vibrate and express from this new frequency; this is being in alignment. Changing our frequency is aligning our vibration on another dimension, the God plane, which is the plane of Love and Light.

This shift in frequency will change us. It will also bring up issues and beliefs that no longer serve us to allow us to acknowledge our past behaviors and to heal. This gives us an opportunity to release and clear out our system. Changing our frequency is not an intellectual process; it encompasses our totality: mind, body, and soul. Think of the tuning fork. When we strike a tuning fork, it vibrates at a certain frequency, and that frequency flows outward, usually in sound. The sound is heard by everyone within hearing distance. The same analogy can be applied to what happens to those around us when our frequency changes. Those around us will hear our sound, the sound of Love.

The reason we do this work on ourselves is not for material gain but to change the world. Lately the news is reporting a trend in mass shootings. One of these events was a mass shooting in a gay bar in Orlando in June of 2016. It was an attack on those who were sexually aligned as LGBTQ. There has been much speculation on the motive of the Orlando shooter. The speculation runs from his having an alliance to ISIS on one end of the spectrum, to the issue of his own personal struggle regarding his sexuality. Many attendees of the gay nightclub suggested that the shooter was a regular there and on homosexual dating apps.

From an outside observer it would be easy to call this a hate crime. Let's face it, the LGBTQ community was targeted. But I think the deeper issue is his deep self-hatred and the tyranny of religious abuse that has affected many of us. We cannot point the finger of blame at one specific religion, because if we did point our finger, it would require us to point our finger at so many other religions that say homosexuality is an abomination. It is daunting to be gay while attempting to deny it in every fiber of your being so that you can belong to a religion, family, or a community. The cognitive dissonance this creates within an individual is really painful.

But if we are free to question our beliefs instead of adhering to another's belief, then we are free to be in the question, to be in the not knowing. Without a sense of certainty, we are able to be in the dialogue with each other in many ways. Without the certainty that we're right and you're wrong, we have the ability to tolerate each other's differences. Without certainty, we can question the reality of heaven or hell; we can question our life purpose; and we can even question politics—all without violence. It's in our ability to question ourselves that we find love and enlightenment.

Imagine if the Orlando shooter was not forced into denying his sexuality, not told by family and religion that his sexuality was against God. What if he knew he was loved, a Divine being? What could he have become if he awakened to his divinity? What would all his victims have been allowed to do as they embraced their life purpose?

Being the frequency of Love allows us to accept all things as possible and accept each other as worthy. It means that we recognize that we are of God, and therefore we can love as God loves. Accepting the possibility that God is Unconditional Love and we are of God allows us to love unconditionally too. Loving unconditionally means you value all human life unequivocally. This isn't about valuing life only when it's within a female's womb, but it's about valuing all life regardless of religion, race, culture, ethnicity, political party. This may sound like an impossible way of being, but it is possible.

It is time for us to put our souls' needs as the priority of our lives. We have placed so much emphasis on our physical comfort and safety, that at times we may have neglected our life purpose, which is to unfold our divinity. While I call for our soul to be a priority, it doesn't mean that we go back to the time period when spiritual fulfillment meant we denied our bodies. This is a call to wake up.

We are Divine human beings, incarnating to experience ourselves as an aspect of God expressing as humankind, while figuring out the truth: we are not separated from the creator or each other. Any belief in separation is a myth and furthers the ideology that there are some people of worth, while thinking there are other people who are unworthy.

Christ Consciousness is the vibration of God being manifested. Yes, I said Christ Consciousness; it is the same as saying Divine human or higher self. Christ is derived from the Greek word *Christos*, which means the anointed one. Christ Consciousness, the Divine human, the anointed human, like each of us, existed before the incarnation of Jesus. Jesus is associated as the Christ because he was seen as the messiah of his people. The teachings of Jesus were the perfect expression of the Christ Consciousness. We can embrace the terms Christ, Divine idea, divinity, etc. in a new way, with a new understanding without past religious teachings triggering us unnecessarily.

It is often said there is only one God and we are all one, that there are no differences between each other. But what do your actions say? Do you behave with love and respect to everyone you meet? If not, then your belief is inaccurate, and it may be the belief you would like to embody, but aren't there in consciousness yet. It's so much easier to stay asleep in consciousness and be comfortable. To change the world, you must awaken to your divinity, and to do so is to tune into the frequency of Love. What if the term the Second Coming of Christ really means the second opportunity of awakening your Christ Consciousness?

In order for our Divine alignment to take place, we must look at our belief systems and fears. Fear is what blocks us and sabotages our lives. We have to clear out these fears and false beliefs to become what we always have been, Divine, Christed. We are here to release past injuries to become aligned to God/Love, which causes our frequency to rise up and for us to live at a higher vibration.

Unconditional Love is not tied to an individual's thoughts or behavior. Unconditional Love simply exists because we exist. I don't know about you, but for me that's a game changer. *It changes everything I believed God to be, and more importantly how I had to think, act, believe to be with God.* This gives me permission to re-evaluate what is sacred versus church doctrine. It gives me permission to see each person regardless of their beliefs as holy and worthy. It allows me to love people who think, feel, and are different than I am. A burden has truly been lifted by this new awakening. I no longer need to save anyone's soul. I no longer need to tell people what is right or wrong. I am free to enjoy their unique gifts and ideas.

What would your world be like if you could just be Unconditional Love and receive Unconditional Love, no matter what you thought or did? Now inevitably when I posit this ideology, I'm asked what about child molesters, rapists, and murderers. Surely, they don't deserve Unconditional Love. My answer has evolved to this response, "Yes, they deserve Unconditional Love and are also accountable for their actions."

Our ability to love is not conditional on someone's behavior, whether it's positive or negative behavior. Saying someone is worthy of being loved unconditionally doesn't mean we support harmful behavior. It simply means we hold their essence as divinity expressing even if they have forgotten the truth of who they are. It also doesn't mean we need to be with someone who is abusive, either, because if we love ourselves unconditionally, then we know our worth and how we wish to be treated. We can love them and choose *not* to be with them.

IT'S JUST AN ILLUSION

The illusion of any "us versus them" ideology is based on fear and lack. The overriding perception in this belief is that there isn't enough for all of us, that there are those taking away from us and that our very survival is at stake by those other people. This then creates a sense of entitlement by those who have, and they often feel it is imperative to keep the status quo. It becomes a way of operating in our systems that supports the myths of some lives are valuable and not others. Believing and supporting this illusion creates the very thing we fear. Separation and violence.

Separation then becomes the norm. Oppression of those not seen as valuable is necessary to continue keeping the false illusion alive. Oppression creates injustice, injustice creates hatred, and hatred creates anarchy. If we treat people as subhuman or worthless, those people start to believe that is their truth. People who believe they are worthless start behaving as though they are worth less. The behaviors of worthless people are filled with violence against the self, then violence against those who oppress. This then becomes a self-fulfilling prophecy through our *isms*, thoughts, perceptions and becomes the world we create. A world of separation filled with "us versus them." An illusion becomes our reality.

The way to transmute this false reality into a world where all are valued is by being the frequency of Love. We are each born from cosmic energy; our essence is of God, God as the energy of Unconditional Love. *This is our Truth, we are a Divine being having a human experience.* Therefore, our natural inclination is to be Unconditional Love. There is this wisdom saying, "Once a man, twice a child." That's usually been interpreted to symbolize the cycle from birth to death. As we watch our parents and grandparents age and become physically weaker, we see them needing care and assistance as they become frail, as children are fragile when they enter our plane of existence.

We can also interpret this wisdom saying in a new way, from the clarity of our spiritual essence. It could be posited that as children we know we are Unconditional Love until we are taught otherwise. Then, as adults, our evolution is about breaking through the illusions of separation, while returning to our Truth: we are Unconditional Love. But in our return to Truth, we are wiser, powerful, and have the ability to transform the world by creating a reality based in Truth.

In our second childhood, we could shift the consciousness of this planet from unawakened to awakened healers. We would act from a place of love, wisdom, and grace. We would be willing to challenge the status quo with love, not violence. We would be willing to look at our beliefs, and change those that no longer serve us with courage, not fear. We would be free to analyze the systems that are in place to help us navigate our culture and determine whether they are still helpful or no longer useful. We would be able to discern new ways of living that work for all sentient beings. We would be able to do all this and more with kindness and dignity.

Being the frequency of Love is not a weak stance; it's a powerful and courageous position of creation. Creation occurs when our hearts are open; destruction happens when our hearts are closed. When our hearts are closed and filled with fear, we rip families and nations apart. When our hearts are open, we value and care for each other, building beautiful communities and wonders. Creation is the act of inventing, producing, making. It's taking the intangible, thoughts, ideas and creating form. Creation alleviates pain; destruction causes pain. Love is an expansive and creative energy. Fear is a constricted and destructive energy.

The power is in the now. We cannot do anything about the past or about the future. All we have is now. In this now moment, we get to choose if we are expressing as our highest form or not. In this now moment, we get to choose to love others and be the frequency of Love. In this now moment, we get to choose to heal our body/relationships/soul/mind. All change happens now.

We can allow ourselves to become hijacked over the smallest things. I have used some terms within this book that seem to be from traditional Christianity. But I hope you are noticing the definitions are not the same. For example, Christ Consciousness from a traditional belief system refers to the consciousness of Jesus after his crucifixion when he arose up in body on the third day. The traditional understanding is that everyone who wants to live eternally must go through the Christ to get to the Father (God)...that's traditional Christianity.

However, I use the term Christ Consciousness to mean the Divine spark within you, Divine consciousness. The Christ or Christ Consciousness has no religious affiliation, no denomination, no sect. I use terms that we may have internalized in a negative connotation to enable us to change our understanding of erroneous beliefs. If each time we hear a term or phrase that causes us to constrict, we are being hijacked on some level of our unconsciousness. Our job is to unearth those terms and create new meanings for ourselves. We have the power to change, create, and reclaim a term, phrase, or concept back from any abuse or negativity. Anytime we shy away from negative terms or concepts, or label it bad, we are giving that belief power and we are living in separation.

My old belief that I could not take care of myself drove me to be in unhealthy relationships, jobs, and situations. It wasn't until I cleared out my false notion of self that I was able to transform. When I am asked about my past, it feels as if that was another person, another lifetime ago. I have been reborn, and I am in my second awakening. My past is mostly discarded, and it feels as though I have been reincarnated anew in this lifetime, my own personal resurrection.

The work being discussed is about healing, including, and transcending. This process can be uncomfortable, and you may feel anxious. But that's normal; you are doing something you've never done before. The paradigms you have used to navigate the world no longer apply. Spiritual work does not have the same rules as navigating systems. The prevalent myth about spiritual development or shifting consciousness is that it has to be done perfectly or with absolute purity. That is erroneous thinking.

Spiritual development and growth are about allowing yourself to be imperfect, to flounder, to feel uncomfortable. This work starts with you! If you don't allow yourself to be imperfect and fumble around, then how can you ever allow your spouse, your parents, or your friends to evolve and change? Spiritual growth requires failure, imperfection; it is not about getting it "right."

Now you may disagree, possibly even say, "I'm a tough critic on myself but not on others." At least that's what I used to say, until I realized the perfectionism I held for myself became projections of my expectations of how other people should live their lives and how other people should interact with me. Still don't believe me? Ask yourself how many times you have thought this question when interacting with others whom you thought didn't behave appropriately, "Were you raised by wolves?" In that question is the inference that they are lacking in social etiquette, or lacking in the way they responded to you. It is a criticism and judgment of the individual.

This is why it's so important to allow yourself to be imperfect. Practice and embrace *imperfect spirituality*! As we shift into this new way of being, we will emanate a new level of acceptance with people in our lives. The frequency of Love is being awake, aware, and accepting. As you resonate in this frequency, you will impact people in ways you couldn't even imagine.

Today I choose to live my life from the understanding of God expressing as Unconditional Love. I choose not to buy into the illusion of separation from God or others. I choose where I put my focus, as opposed to being hijacked by my fear-based thoughts. I am loved and worthy, solely because I exist, a Divine human being. Each of us has our own stuff to work through, sometimes it is accomplished with grace and dignity, other times it looks a hot mess. I'll be honest, there are times when my energetic shifts aren't graceful. But I also trust my next shift will be quicker and easier to transform the more I become adept at aligning with the Christ.

However it manifests, there is no blame or shame. I choose to release expectations, disappointment, anger, and hatred. I affirm our life events are creations for us to learn, grow, and evolve. What are you aligning yourself to—to the status quo, to your role, to your class, to your sexuality, to your race or gender, to being comfortable? My beloved, *change* is the awakening. Now is the time.

Chapter 9

Truth by Any Name is Still Truth

There is a sense that we are living in a period of time in which we have the capacity to evolve to a higher level of consciousness and we are being given many opportunities. We have seen in the last century many teachings that have been downloaded to us in a myriad of ways. Many of these messages resonate within us on a molecular level and open our self-awareness. The messengers have names such as Emma Curtis Hopkins, Edgar Cayce, Charles and Myrtle Fillmore, Mary Baker Eddy, Helen Schucman and William Thetford, Ernest Holmes, Bill W., and Dr. Bob, and many others.

When we listen to these teachings, it can be difficult to figure out what's truth. *Truth can be defined as the unchanging spiritual reality.* But if we believe in One Presence and One Power, then we know even if a teaching is not Truth, it can still be valuable for where we are on our journey.

Truth is defined in the dictionary as something that is in accordance with fact or reality, a fact or belief that is accepted as true. Let's make the distinction between our own individual truth and the Spiritual Truth. The Spiritual Truth is unchangeable, cannot be altered. Spiritual Truth encompasses the Universe; it is not limited to this realm, time, or place. Our truth is always changing because everything in this realm is changeable. Our reality is simply based on our perception of the world. Therefore, my reality may be different than your reality because of our different experiences in the world.

For example, my husband and I navigate the world differently because of our experiences and worldview. When I drive our car in US States that have a policy of racial profiling, I am on high alert. As a woman of mixed heritage, my truth says, I will be targeted to be pulled over and harassed. However, my hubby's experiences, as a white European male, are not the same. He drives our car as he normally does. He's not worried that if he follows the rules of the road he could be pulled over. His truth is if he obeys the laws there is no reason for a police officer to pull us over. In the early years of our marriage I would fuss with him about how "clueless" he could be, but he wasn't. His truth is simply different than mine. Our truth often comes down to our experiences and perceptions of what is happening.

With this in mind, we can realize we have the power to change our reality by changing our perceptions. I no longer fuss with my hubby or think he is clueless. I get that his worldview will differ from mine. Also, I realized it's been about fifteen years since I've been pulled over and harassed by a racist officer. This made me question my own belief about being a target. Now I drive as I previously did, following the rules of the road, but with a sense of deserving and belonging. We are cocreators by the thoughts, words, and feelings held in mind that we allow to become our reality.

Do you think that believing we are small and limited is Truth? You are not incomplete; you are whole. Stop comparing your failures to someone else's successes. We each have unique gifts. It's time to stop searching outside of ourselves for fulfillment, for love, for safety. All the searching to find ourselves is really about you needing you...you needing your own self-love. Every time we search outside ourselves for someone to love us, protect us, see us, we are really looking for *us to love us, us to protect us, and us to see the amazing unique Divine human being that we already are.*

Each time we search outside for something or someone to complete us, we have given up our power as a creator. We then have given that power to the one we seek. Each time you hear a fearmonger say the world is a dangerous place and you agree with them, you are cocreating a fearful society. Then if you also look to the same fearmonger for protection, you are creating in fear and creating systems that are filled with injustice. Any thoughts created outside of Love are created from fear. Most of our civilized systems were created from a place of fear. The penal system in the United States has been created from fear.

You may say you didn't create that horrible system. But I remind you every time you are silent or comply, you are in agreement with the system. The US has the highest percentage of incarcerated people in the world. The largest groups incarcerated are Black men, followed by Latin men. The largest-growing populations in the jail system are Black women. Why? Fear! Think about this: when you think of being attacked or stolen from or a crime being perpetrated by someone, what color is that someone? For many of us, the perpetrator is someone of color. We live in a culture in which we are continually told what to think, whom to believe, what's right, and what's wrong. When we look at the story lines perpetuated by television, movies, and the media, we are bombarded by "others" doing bad things to us. Those others are usually people who are of color.

We cannot help but have unconscious biases; it's been programmed in us for a very long time. We buy into the need for protection from those "others." We buy into the myth that there are those who are deserving and those who are not. Many of our created systems mirror and propagate this belief. Even systems as basic as education or healthcare are created from a place of fear, not love. And each time we are silent, we are in agreement with the system. It's our responsibility to discern whether to continue the systems as they are or to change them or to dismantle them.

There is no "they" who will do it for us. Once we change our programming, our beliefs, the out-picturing of the world must change accordingly.

The antidote to creating in fear is to create from the now moment because right now you are safe. Anytime you feel anxious or afraid become aware that you are out of the present moment. Because in this moment, you are safe, you are free. The more of those safe moments we create from the more we create a world that is safe for everyone.

You always have the choice to discern if what someone speaks is Truth. You always have the choice to believe what someone says or thinks about you. You always have a choice to take what people say to heart and make it personal. The truth is that any time you agree with what someone says or does, you are embracing their belief system as Truth. If someone insults you and you have hurt feelings about it, then you have agreed that their perception of you is Truth. We know that the human condition can be mercurial at times. Someone may be having a good day, vibrating as the frequency of Love and seeing beauty and goodness in everyone and everything. Yet if that same person is having a day where they are feeling fearful or angry, they are more likely going to spew words of discord.

It's up to us whether we take in their perception and beliefs as our own. It's up to us to believe the limited thoughts we have internalized from listening to others as a definition of who we are. Right now you can challenge your own mind-set, you can ask yourself, "Is this what I really believe about myself, or is it something someone else has told me, something I have internalized as myself?" If the answer is "This isn't who I am," then create a new belief system about yourself. (Q7)

PROSPERITY/ABUNDANCE/ENOUGH

"Poverty is missing the mark; it's an erroneous concept of living a spirit-filled life." – Rev. Sheree

What if all substance of the Universe resides in you? How powerful would you feel? If we really believed that we are the expression of Allness, then we would know we could do all that Jesus, Muhammad (pbuh), Buddha, and Krishna have done. No, we could do greater things than these masters. But we don't seem to be able to even match what they did. Why? The one-word answer is Faith. Let's define faith.

Faith is defined today as a system of religious belief, a belief that is not based on proof, confidence or trust in a person or thing, the obligation of loyalty. Etymologically, (the origin of a word and historical development of its meaning), the word faith is derived from the Greek word *peitho*, which means "to persuade," from which derives the spiritual meaning of faith "divine persuasion." Secularly, in the Ancient Near East, faith meant a guarantee. Metaphysically, faith can be interpreted as consciousness centered in God/Love.

Is it possible to make a correlation that faith can be seen as a guarantee that we can do all things when we are centered in the flow of Love? The answer is yes, if we come to the understanding that faith isn't magical or an impetus for a deity to answer our desires. Faith is simply being steeped in the conscious flow of Divine Love.

Faith is an act; we make a decision to turn it on. Think about turning on the lights in your home. You just know that electricity is there to support the lights being turned on. It's the same concept for being in the divine flow, this energy and substance is always there, ever present. There is nothing to go and get, nothing to become, nothing to work harder at. It is simply the realization that we have it all already within us and we believe from, not believe in, something outside of us. If we believe from within that we are limited and not enough, then we manifest a life of limitations and lack. But if we believe from the *kingdom* within us – and act in faith, then we are capable of manifesting abundance, greatness.

All this time that we have railed against the unfairness of the world and our lives, we could have been creating abundance instead. Because when we perceive our lives as being unfair, we are not living life from within out. We are living life from victimhood and powerlessness. I understand that the majority of us have been taught that success is measured from the outside in. We have been taught from childhood that only a teacher's evaluation of us as an A or B student is perceived as a child being successful. From our earliest memories, we have been conditioned to believe that success means we have lots of material things, accolades, awards, respect, and deference from others, etc. But I'm reminding you again living life from the outside in is not what you incarnated here to be.

Let's take a moment to deconstruct the word prosperity. If you look at any dictionary today, prosperity is usually tied to financial success. But if one studies the etymology of the word, prosperity comes from the fourteenth-century Latin root word *prosperus*, which means "according to one's hope or expectation."

In today's vernacular, the word abundance means affluence, wealth, as well as overflowing fullness. However, culturally we associate the word abundance to mean one who has a large quantity of riches or wealth. Etymologically the word abundance came from the fourteenth-century Latin root word *abundantia*, which means fullness, plenty, to overflow. The final word we will define is substance; it is defined today as that of which a thing consists; physical matter or material. This word comes from twelfth-century Latin *substantia*, which means being, essence, material, to stand under, to be present.

When I use the term substance, I am talking about Divine substance; this is the essence of everything we are and what the Universe is made of. The next question is, where does this substance come from? I think we can agree God is *not* a deity sitting on a heavenly throne dispensing this thing called substance. Substance is simply the Allness that we move and live in and flows through our being. It's about understanding that the Universe/God is simply the essence and frequency of Love.

Once we keep ourselves centered on the truth that Love is the essence of the Universe, we are then open to be able to recognize the abundance of the Universe. This recognition enables us to realize we are a part of all things. Being in the Divine flow (Love) allows us to acknowledge the limitlessness of who we can become, of the ever-present substance, and then recognize we can shape this substance to be the natural way of expressing. True prosperity and abundance, according to one's hope of fullness can only come from living life from the belief of the kingdom of riches are within you.

Remember this book's premise is about living our lives from the inside out. But still we work so hard to camouflage what we feel, believe, and fear from ourselves and others. As we start using techniques to help us change our perceptions, we use affirmations and visualizations in an attempt to change our limiting beliefs and then get frustrated when they don't work like we think they are supposed to. Why aren't they working?

Rev. Eric Butterworth, in his book *Spiritual Economics*, writes, *"This is the common confusion about the practice of affirmative prayer, that if you speak the words of Truth over and over, you impress them on the subconscious mind and thus they become true for you. They do not become true because you affirm them. You affirm them because they are true. You are synchronizing your consciousness with the reality of Truth, creating a channel through which the mystical flow may do its powerful work through you."*

If you are reading this book, I know you have done some self-awareness work already and have taken onboard many spiritual practices such as meditation, affirmations, denials, visualizations, embracing positivity, yoga, etc. And many of you may be thinking, "Of course, I knew that and approached prosperity consciousness in this way. I worked from synchronizing my consciousness with Truth and still my life isn't reflecting prosperity. Why?!!" The answer is simple:

"You cannot create from rejecting who you are." – Rev. Sheree

If you believe that you are not enough, not of Love, then how could you create anything other than lack? Anything manifesting from a rejection of self cannot be abundance or prosperity. It's counterintuitive; it's against how spiritual laws work. It is imperative we honor that we are divine and beautifully made. We must come to embrace all aspects of self to claim our divine inheritance. It is time to be the expression of the Universe and know the Universe is designed to support you. This is a spiritual law and unchangeable.

The issues of lack happen when we don't believe this Truth, when all we see are our limitations and name them unholy. We then make an attempt to eradicate those aspects of self. It's like telling the Universe it made trash when you were created. Of course, believing about ourselves as less than, we cannot help but manifest a life of limit and lack. Because when we believe that we are not enough, unworthy, [insert your own label here], then we have cut ourselves off from the Divine flow.

God/Source/Love/Universe/Allness cannot supply lack. This is because lack is a state of mind (a belief or worldview). To change from the belief in lack, we must instill spiritual practices in our lives to assist us in helping to change our beliefs. This is also why I write so frequently on acknowledging the truth of what we are, divinity, and raising our consciousness. These two aspects are the key to our abundance and prosperity. We are Divine, special, anointed. By raising our consciousness, we become expansive, we recognize we are entitled to the abundance and support of the Universe. That is getting into the flow.

Once we are in the flow, it's not about gaining money or material things. It's about being an awakened consciousness that resides in the flow and allowing it to support you in all your needs. The difficulty is it's so easy to forget this truth when we reside on the Earth plane. This is why we frequently practice being in the presence of divinity through exercises like meditation and prayer, just to be in the flow of God and the kingdom within.

Stop trying to make a demonstration, a miracle, happen. In the Universe all things are possible. A miracle suggests something magical or an intervention. What do you believe is real? Is it what you see with your human eyes and the things the experts tell you are real, or do you see your reality from the light of the kingdom within? In my own personal experience, when I believed in my inability to care for myself, it was inevitable that I would become out of work. I also believed the experts who said the economy was on the fritz and that the only way corporations could be healthy was to terminate thousands of employees.

This worry, in essence, became my manifestation because unknowingly my underlying belief system was using the law of visualization. Remember I keep saying life is lived from within out. My focus at that time was on my external worries, which then became the outward life I would live. The law of visualization is a spiritual law, when used correctly is focused in the Divine flow. Your consciousness sees spiritual substance available for you to manifest whatever you need. Then, from being in the flow, one draws all one needs for health, wealth, and wisdom without losing one's Truth.

Please understand this: money is not real wealth. Rather it is a device for measuring wealth. This means culturally we have given the concept of money power. Too little money means I'm a failure, not good enough, or even the misconception of "spiritual." Too much money means I'm valued and entitled. We have allowed money to define our worth, value, success. But truly the reality is that money is neutral or innocent. It's the energy we and the collective unconscious create about money that makes it so debilitating or vital to so many.

Money is the symbol of the idea of prosperity. So having created a tangible out-picturing of substance allows us to create an economy in which we place our trust based on the reality of money. If I want a service or product from you, the exchange of money allows us to have cooperation. I will have the product I want, and you will have prosperity symbolized by the money I have given to you. There is a sense of trust that we have an even playing field.

If money is a symbol of spiritual substance in form, then where do we get ideas that money defines us, tells us our worth or success? We get this belief about money from our culture, families, friends, and our childhood, adolescence, and adult experiences with money. Money just is, not good or bad, not about your survival or well-being. I say this because money is a construct. It's a concept that we were taught has meaning for our survival.

We bought into the collective unconscious that we can justify most things if it means we can obtain money/wealth. We have bought into the construct that money has more value than human life. One only has to look at the choices governments and corporations make that put money as the most important thing over human life. We even go to war and kill people for economic reasons.

When you focus solely on visualizing for material wealth, you lose your center and become someone who worships things. Visualizing for material things means one's focus becomes the riches and wealth on this plane, as opposed to knowing the kingdom of riches are within you and of the Universe. It becomes a matter of throwing away your Divine inheritance for "money." What I'm talking about is "true seeing." Seeing from within and releasing the view that others have created as your reality. When we see from within, we see the reality of light, love, abundance. This is how we cocreate.

Let's be clear, this is not about reconditioning our minds to believe everything is "all good." The "all good" mantra is an attempt to convince ourselves that whatever the situation, we will be okay. Usually this is coming from an attempt to change our thoughts from negativity or fear to positivity. We have gotten used to saying and thinking these positive phrases because we think that's what Truth students do. But if we are doing this from our humanness, we are limited. It's not a matter of doing; it's a matter of being. Us being in the flow of the infinite, syncing in with God/Love/Light as who we are, who we have come here to be.

By keeping ourselves focused and centered on our Divine inheritance, we become abundance. This is prosperity consciousness. We create from our beliefs and world perceptions. Whatever is created in your life today is not from things you see outside, but from how you see yourself. This is about being authentic to yourself, not trying to be something you are not. You are beautifully made in your own right. There is no need to recreate ourselves into something or someone else.

If you don't like who you are, that makes it difficult. You may make attempts to change yourself into what you think you should be, but that won't work if you are coming from a place of self-rejection. Who do you say you are? Not enough, poor, without a degree, unlucky? I tell you, you are made of the starlight of the cosmos; you are a Divine human being. I am simply reminding you of your Truth: the kingdom of riches is within you, because this is the core of everything, of our lives. If we do not believe this, then it is pointless. You are the "I am" of the Universe, the image of the Universe expressing. You are the expression of God-mind, and it's only from this reality that you are healthy, wealthy, and wise.

As an eternal being, we know we have incarnated to raise our consciousness, to be able to overcome our egoic needs for truth. As a spiritual being, it's always about unfolding our highest self, no matter where we incarnate. We are here to overcome the limitations of this world and culture to do great things. Faith is saying yes to the Truth of what you are. Faith is saying yes to the kingdom of riches within. Faith is saying yes to living life from the inside out. Faith is saying yes to being in the flow of Source. Faith is saying yes to an abundant life. Faith is saying yes to love. It is that simple if we allow it to be. When we say yes, the Universe conspires with us. The steps to take become clear; there is no need to figure it out.

How do we build our awareness? Through the act of gratitude! Gratitude is an act that we can take to bring our awareness to the abundance that is our lives. Now I know this sounds cliché, but it's a powerful state of consciousness that gives us a boost into the flow of abundance. When I am in the consciousness of gratitude, my energy is off the chart. There is a whirlwind of vitality, hope, possibilities, and sureness in my step. This is what draws abundance to us. One only needs the desire to feel grateful.

An example could look like this: I bought my new car, and I'm filled with gratitude that I have a reliable car that is comfortable, has lots of electronics, and I love the color. It's a burnt-orange color. Every place I drive I see that car/color, it sticks out like a neon sign. This occurs because in my case I am grateful for this car and I am aware of this blessing, hence, my subconscious mind sees it all the time. What we become aware of we see everywhere we go. In this example, it's the blessing of this car.

The meaning to bless can be defined as "to confer prosperity upon," first coined by Rev. Eric Butterworth. He suggested that it is from a grateful mind and heart that we can confer prosperity upon our lives, friends, family, neighbors, drivers next to us, folks on line at the grocery store, etc. Why do we want to confer a blessing on what we see? It's a shift of our awareness, moving from lack consciousness to abundance. If we look for the blessing, we find the blessing.

We can make a conscious choice to see the world as it is—no judgment, no label. We can center ourselves in the flow of substance and sync our consciousness in abundance. We can even take it a step further and bless others. Now it's not the Southern version of "bless your heart," because you know it doesn't mean the same thing. "Bless your heart" is a gentle way of saying, "Poor thing, you are clueless."

When we bless someone, we confer prosperity upon them. We put our energy, consciousness, and love into that blessing. We are here to be a blessing to each other. Start to change your consciousness today. Wherever you go, whomever you meet, in your mind I want you to bless them, or even better, speak these words to them, "I bless you. I confer prosperity upon you."

JOY IS YOUR BIRTHRIGHT

There is a myth in New Age Positivity Tradition that if we hold in our consciousness and speak only positive thoughts that our lives will be magically wonderful and we become abundant. And when the outward manifestation of our lives doesn't reflect prosperity, joy, hope, health, etc., there is an outcry from ourselves and others of spiritual malpractice. We may say or hear phrases such as: "You know you manifested this" or "You didn't regularly practice meditation and prayer" or "You're not spiritual or positive enough."

Possibly we say these things to those we see as "failing in transformation" from a place of our own confusion, helpfulness, and fear. Because our mind may believe that if this could happen to him/her, then it could happen to us. Therefore, we hold on to the myth that there is some kind of formula we can live by to feel in control. The reality is there is no formula. Living is filled with change. Is being filled with negative thoughts destructive? Yes. But it takes more than just having positive thoughts to change our lives for the better. We must also align with the knowing of our Truth as a Divine human being, while we hold positive thoughts *and* are present to fully feeling and being with what is.

Joy and happiness are something we all seem to want and strive for. Yet joy doesn't come from striving. Joy comes from being attuned to our natural rhythm for rest and relaxation. How many times do we crow, "I'm so busy" or "Life is so busy"? We say it as a badge of honor. As if being busy implies we are so valued, needed, and important. The unsaid thinking is that being busy means we are successful.

Wayne Muller in his book *Sabbath: Finding Rest, Renewal, and Delight in Our Busy Lives* writes about our cultural perception of success.

> "A 'successful' life has become a violent enterprise. We make war on our own bodies, pushing them beyond their limits; war on our children, because we cannot find enough time to be with them when they are hurt and afraid, and need our company; war on our spirit, because we are too preoccupied to listen to the quiet voices that seek to nourish and refresh us; war on our communities, because we are fearfully protecting what we have, and do not feel safe enough to be kind and generous; war on the earth, because we cannot take the time to place our feet on the ground and allow it to feed us, to taste its blessings and give thanks."

The really interesting thing is that this being busy has an underlying ethos of fear. As if we pause for mindfulness or rest, we fear we will no longer be needed or matter. We have been conditioned to accomplish, be productive, and consume. The accepted norm is that we must continuously strive to be successful; anything else means failure. If we are busy consuming, doing, getting, then when do we have time for joy?

Joy comes from the wellspring within. This wellspring is replenished by rest, mindfulness, and relaxation. The overworked, overresponsible, overaccumulating, overwanting life we live is taxing to our bodies, minds, and souls.

The need to rest is normal, and yet there is such resistance in our psyche to allow ourselves this rest. Is there a part of ourselves that we equate quiet and stillness with emptiness? Is there fear that if we stop for long enough we may feel that aching void within us, which may seem like never-ending neediness that we fill with tasks, jobs, work, to-dos. But what if that void is where we birth our creativity and wisdom. The breath of God needs that void to breathe us.

Right here and right now is a defining moment for us. We can decide to challenge the belief that our success comes from the almost desperate acts of nonstop activity. How many times have we said to ourselves, "When I'm retired, thin, kids are grown, move, divorce, get married...then I'll be able to be joyful." The time to be happy is now. It's up to us to make the decision that joy is our birthright, and we can be bubbling with joy now, not someday or one day.

In the New Testament we can find confirmation of our birthright in Galatians 5:22-23: "By contrast, the fruit of the Spirit is love, joy, peace, patience, kindness, generosity, faithfulness, gentleness, and self-control. There is no law against such things."

Galatians is a letter the Apostle Paul has written to the people of Galatia. He is reminding them of their truth. Paul is saying to those who have embraced this new level of awakened consciousness, they do not need to be concerned about what others say is truth or the law. He is reminding the Galatians that they are called to a new freedom. Paul gives the metaphor of fruit trees to symbolize that by being aligned in the Christ Frequency, they automatically receive spiritual gifts.

Fruit trees can bear only the fruit they are created to produce. An apple tree will bear only apples. So when Paul speaks of the fruit of the Spirit, we can infer that once we align with our Truth that we are spiritual human beings, we can only bear fruits of the Spirit. It implies that we don't have to do anything special, because as Divine beings, Spirit is the essence of what we are.

Hence, it is natural for us to be joy-filled. We don't have to work for joy. The more we claim our divinity, the larger and sweeter our fruits grow. The only thing we need to do is allow Spirit to work through us and we cannot help but bear these fruits.

Now that we have determined that joy is within each of us, let's look at what practical steps we can do to help us remember. First, we can create a new story. The new story we create could look like this: part of a successful life is being able to rest, relax, and take care of ourselves. The new mantra we can use to anchor this within our awareness: *I am willing to create a wellspring of joy through rest and self-care.*

The time to allow our wellspring to fill is now. Imagine cultivating a source of unlimited joy through rest and relaxation. Once we make the decision that the time for joy is now, we can boost our joy by starting our day with gratitude. Being in a state of gratitude has amazing benefits to our well-being. Upon awakening we can start the day by being grateful for a good night's sleep, running water, love, a/c, sunshine, etc. Thinking of the reasons to be grateful allows us to prime our hearts to see the good. Gratitude also allows us to realize we are enough and have enough. Knowing that we are sufficient gives way to allowing for more rest and relaxation in our lives. When we are in gratitude consciousness, we are focused on our gifts, not in lack or comparison. The gifts of gratitude allow us to prime our system for joy to bubble and overflow in our lives.

Next, let go of what's not working. For example, if your list of things to do is growing and your joy is diminishing, stop writing the list. I don't know about you, but I don't want my obituary to say "She completed her list." I want to be known for living life to the fullest, being kind and loving to all I meet, inspiring joy in life's small moments. My suggestion is to release things that are no longer important and no longer vital to do, step out into nature, play, sing, dance, or call that person you have wanted to talk to for a while.

Try being kind to yourself and others. Joy grows through kindness. If I'm unable to be kind to myself, I don't have a shot at being kind to anyone else. When I'm demonstrating kindness, it taps into my wellspring, and a by-product is joy. Compliment yourself...children already understand this; they have a knack for celebrating all the little things they are and do. Give yourself the gift of wonder. Some of my most joyful moments have come from being silly, and sometimes joy fills my soul over something as small as taking a moment to watch a lightning bug or sunset.

Other tips for becoming joyous: be what you are, Love. See the love in your interactions with others; bless them with love or prosperity by beaming that energy to them. Allow your inner child to make choices from your heart. Compliment a stranger, pay it forward. Allow grace to drive your words and actions, give yourself and others the benefit of not judging. Look through their opinions and see their rightness. This may sound like a small thing, but when we see the divinity and rightness of ourselves, we are happy. And when we see the divinity and rightness of others, we honor them and elicit their joy!

Another way to commit to being joyous in life is to step into your calling. There is no need to wait for the right time. The right time is now. Moving into your life purpose can be done in small increments. A first step can be as simple as having informational chats with folks who may be doing something similar to your dream. It could be meditating about what the possibilities could look like if you were to take a baby-step approach. Find a mentor and ask for help. Claim what is your passion. When we are doing what we are spiritually, emotionally, intellectually called to do, we beam with so much joy and love, it is contagious.

Chapter 10

Now What?

POSITIVE STEPS TO HELP OTHERS

Many of us want to take steps to help others. But before we can launch into this endeavor, we have to help ourselves first. It is only from a place of recognizing our true riches that we can make the world around us transform. I don't know about you, but I cannot be joy-filled and overflowing if I'm focused on lack, because when I'm in lack, I'm in the space of need. One cannot give if one is in need. Any attempt at giving from that space dries up the energetic flow of abundance, because when we give from lack, we give from fear and resentment.

As richness overflows in your own life, you can't help but share it with others. As light workers— those who care deeply about the world and want to help others—we cannot help but share our riches with others. Of course, it's impossible to share if we believe we don't have. As the song says, "Nothing from nothing leaves nothing, you gotta have something if you want to be with me."

Often we may not see ourselves as rich and abundant. Perhaps it is because we compare ourselves to others, and it always looks better over there. Could we have bought into the belief that to be really spiritual means we abhor money? Perhaps it's simply that we are unable to see our abundance. I have a family member who has not worked in over twenty years, their house is paid in full, all their bills are paid on time, they purchase food and clothing when necessary, and they complain about how poor they are. They call their life hard. They are constantly in a state of need and unable to be kind or generous to others. Once again, it's this person's belief about wealth and poverty that defines their happiness and actions.

There has been so much discussion about those who have and those who have not. Reading the news, there are all manner of studies that suggest the income gap between the wealthy and middle class has become unreachable to bridge. I don't have the answers to change the issue of poverty, but I believe we can do something to alleviate their pain and suffering. We could tap into our resources and leverage them. Our resources are spiritual, intellectual, emotional, and physical. Spiritually we are redefining the essence of who we are: ageless, eternal, whole. There are wisdom and possibilities in us that haven't been fully tapped yet. There is a kingdom of riches within us.

Again I ask you, what do you really believe? Do you recognize that you cocreate the world and have immense power to shape what you see? Our purpose is to realize this and cocreate a world where all beings thrive. From this clarity of Truth, we draw out the good that is there for ourselves and for everyone. One simple step in honoring the good on this journey is to see the wonder in the smallest things and feel the gratitude. Slowly this opens your eyes to see the richness and fullness of your life.

Is it wonderful to have nice things and be surrounded by beauty? Yes, but if that is how we define ourselves as successful, then our intention is out of alignment. Material things are a by-product, not the Truth of who and what we are. I think we may have forgotten that our success is really about the unfolding of our divinity. This unfoldment is our purpose and reason for being. Our purpose is not to accumulate the forms of this realm.

When I mentioned poverty, what feelings or thoughts came to mind? For me, my first thoughts: "How can I tackle something that big, how could I make a difference in folks' lives?" Then this verse came to mind: "For where two or three are gathered in my name, I am there among them." This verse in Matthew 18:20 is written when Jesus is speaking about forgiveness and reconciliation of those who have transgressed against another. And after he speaks of reconciliation, the author of Matthew says Jesus then utters the words, "For where two or three are gathered in my name, I am there among them." The emphasis is the certainty that God/Spirit is present when prayer or meditation is shared with another. From an energetic perspective, this is about the whole being greater than the individual parts. When we come together in sacred prayer, meditation, or service, the power is exponential as opposed to going it alone.

The reality is that we are made in the image and likeness of the Universe. The Universe is set up to give to us. To tap into this flow of abundance, we must emulate the Universe as givers. Life is a giving process. As we evolve in consciousness, we can't help but give. We must express as Divine beings and that is the opposite of being concerned or focused on getting. As we express and give, we can't help but receive. It's just how spiritual laws of giving work.

I did some research and found that there is a model called giving circles that is becoming quite popular in grassroots giving. In the 2016 Nonprofit Quarterly there was an article entitled, "Could Giving Circles Rebuild Philanthropy from the Bottom Up" that described how giving circles work. "Giving circles are voluntary groups that enable individuals to pool their money (and sometimes their time as volunteers) to support organizations of mutual interest. They also provide opportunities for education and engagement among participants about philanthropy and social change, connecting them to charities, their communities, and each other." This allows for members of the circle to collectively discuss and decide where to put their efforts, money, and resources. This is a model for social change at a grassroots level. These circles have a history of supporting women and minorities.

What if you create a giving circle in your community? Get a group of like-minded people to come together, and decide what you can do to affect poverty, homelessness, hunger, and educational options for those who need assistance, right here in our own backyard. The circle can become whatever you wished it to be— for example: for a specific time period making alliances with organizations that choose to share resources. It could even eventually become the model that an awakened movement embraces as we perform sacred service wherever our community resides.

Imagine having an impact on young women becoming powerful leaders and visionaries. Imagine helping a domestic survivor become a business owner who helps other survivors. We can cocreate a world that works for all if we harness the truth of what we are. But we cannot do this from lack consciousness; we can only do amazing things from a consciousness of prosperity.

Right now on our planet, the ideology of "us versus them" is no longer working. We see time and again we are all linked globally. Your refuse becomes our cancer. Our GMO becomes your famine. We cannot only be concerned about our own separate sustainability. *WE ARE NOT SEPARATE FROM EACH OTHER, AND WE ARE NOT SEPARATE FROM GOD!*

We cannot raise our frequency, vibrate at a higher level, and shift our consciousness if we believe in separation from each other or from God. We are the same as indigenous people, white, black, brown, straight, gay, and transgendered. We are the same as those who are educated, uneducated, rich, and poor. We are the same as racists and rapists. We are only at different stages of realizing our Truth. By witnessing each other's Truth and divinity, we have the ability to call each other up higher, and give everyone permission to shift. No one is better than; should you find yourself immersed in that thinking, you have gone out of alignment with your divinity.

The measure of our rise in frequency is not based on comparison or judgment of another. Living as our Christed self is incompatible with hatred, discrimination, and demeaning of others. The moment we say your life is not as valuable as my life, we have stepped out of alignment. Today you have a choice to walk out your door and see each person you meet as their Divine self, or decide to remain unchanged and view the world through the lens of separation.

WHAT ARE YOU WAITING FOR?

This is our time of great awakening! We can no longer play small and be satisfied with it because we know that we are limiting ourselves. We are here to be the powerful beings we are meant to be. What are you waiting for? (Q8)

> Answer: You! You are what you have always been waiting for!!

There is no savior coming to save you, to save your soul and take you to heaven. There is no government that will take care of you. There is no politician who will put your needs first or make you a priority. There is no guru or spiritual leader who is going to guarantee you enlightenment. There is no one else out there who is going to fix you, make you feel better, make you whole.

"In oneself lies the whole world and if you know how to look and learn, the door is there and the key is in your hand. Nobody on earth can give you either the key or the door to open, except yourself." –Jiddu Krishnamurti

You! You are what you have always been waiting for!! You've known this from the time you were born, but it has been easy to forget through the indoctrination by parents, society, teachers, friends, and others who said otherwise. So, if your parents were fearful, they taught you to be fear-filled. If your parents were racist, they taught you to be a racist. If your parents were blaming, then they taught you how to blame. Then, as you grow up, you do the same things as you were taught, maybe to a lesser or higher degree.

Unless you choose to question your beliefs! There is no need to blame anyone for the lessons they taught us; they did it mainly from a place of loving us and wanting us to thrive in our society. Yes, they did the best they knew how from their perceptions of the world, from their own indoctrination. How could they do anything else?

We can decide to continue being in resistance to our childhood and our parents. We can stomp our feet and say we didn't get enough love, support, acceptance, etc. But all unforgiveness does is to keep us in resistance to what was and is. It keeps us stuck and from reaching our Allness and living our life's purpose. So you can continue to keep doing what you've been doing, but that will only keep giving you the same results. Or you can choose to forgive your family/teachers/friends. They may have damaged or abused you or treated you poorly, but they did it from what they experienced, from what they thought was normal.

"When you surrender, you tap into a power greater than your mind, greater than your plans, greater than your ability to comprehend. When you stop trying to control, you are able to tune in to your consciousness...You don't have to drive life. You just have to take your foot off the brake. When you do that, you go beyond the mind, you transcend limited logic. You enter the miracle zone. It's a realm of unlimited possibilities." –*You Are The One* – Kute Blackson

I know you may think—forgiving and surrender is easier said than done. You don't know the horror/apathy/fear I lived. No, I don't know. But I do know that holding on to resentment and anger toward them harms you. So, it depends on what you want your life to be. It's in forgiving them that you'll finally find freedom. Whatever trauma your family/teachers/friends did to you is on them. Whatever they didn't do for you, it's on them. It's theirs to decide to deal with or not. But who you become and the life you live are on you. That's where the power lies.

Are you ready to step into your power and your greatness? (Q9)

Worksheets and Tables and Qs

(Worksheet 1)

Think back to your earliest memories, remember what you felt and how you viewed your world. Take a moment to jot down a few words in the boxes below to describe *your perceptions as a child*, prior to indoctrination:

Childhood Worldview

Place one-word snapshots in any area of the picture. They are part of your treasure chest!

Q1: To begin this journey to awakened awareness, I ask you, will you place your soul in charge of your journey and trust where it leads you?

(Worksheet 2)

Without judgment or criticisms reflect on the *isms* you just read and take personal inventory. What *isms* are you benefiting from? Which *ism* would you like to release? Which *ism* still makes sense to you and you will continue to abide by? Take a moment to go within and write your answers below:

What *isms* are mine to analyze?

(Worksheet 3)
The question is, what are you aligning yourself to—the status quo, your role, your class, your race or gender, being comfortable? Take a moment to reflect and write your answers below:

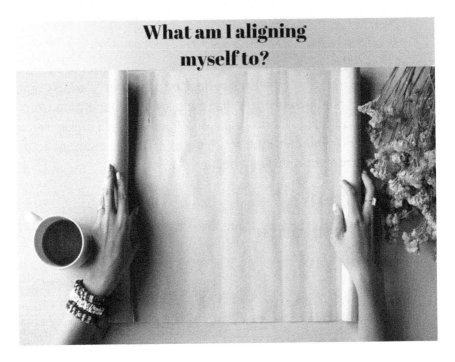

(Worksheet 4)

Take a moment to journal your responses to the following question: What feelings or thoughts came up for you as you completed this exercise?

(Q2) What are your distortions of self? Can you go deeper...past your own feeling of self-dislike...deeper...past your own negative self-perceptions to see the truth of who you are? What are you willing to let go of?

(Worksheet 5)

What do you think about sex? Is sex incompatible with your spirituality? If so, I invite you to explore your beliefs and decide if it is time to shift your perception around your sexuality. What if you embraced your sexuality as a Divine human being? Take a moment to reflect on these questions and write your thoughts below:

My beliefs about sex and God:

(Worksheet 6)

Questions: How do you label the emotion anger? Is it bad? Is it unladylike? Is it needed to be powerful? Is it something you pretend you never experience because you are spiritual? Is it disrespectful? Take a moment to reflect on these questions and jot your answers below:

My beliefs about anger

(Worksheet 7)
The next part of this exercise is to explore what is anger. How does it feel? What are the positive aspects of anger? What are the aspects of anger that can trip you up? Give yourself time to ponder these questions and write your thoughts below:

My anger feels, looks, behaves like:

(Q3) What is the story you tell yourself about aging?

(Table 1)
When we find ourselves in resistance to what is happening now and feeling anxious, we need to shift back to present moment awareness. Here are some tips on how to shift back to the present moment.

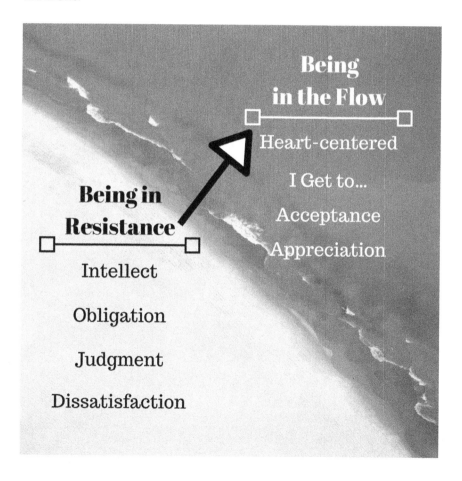

(Worksheet 8)

Write your thought that is causing you cognitive dissonance here:

Decide on the model you want to work with either on the left or right side. Then write down the responses that come to mind in the appropriate box.

Eliminating Cognitive Dissonance

COGNITIVE BEHAVIOR TECHNIQUE	SPIRITUAL PRACTICE
• Trivializing the inconsistency	• There is only one Presence and one Power active as the Universe and as my life, God the Good.
• Adding a thought	• Our essence is of God; therefore, we are inherently good.
• Change in behavior	• We are cocreators with God, creating reality through thoughts held in mind.
• Change in thought	• Through prayer and meditation, we align our heart-mind with God.
	• Through thoughts, words, and actions, we live the Truth we know.

(Worksheet 9)

Rev. Paul Smith has a five-step psychospiritual process to help you build a relationship with God. He calls it "Sitting with Jesus." I suggest you modify this process and call it "Sitting with God/Love/Light/Divinity/etc." The key is that whatever name you use for God is appropriate.

Sitting with God:

1. Welcome the presence of Jesus/God/Divine Feminine/Guides. Thank you, _____ for being here with me. *(Think about what you do when folks visit: you make them feel welcomed, you are happy to see them and tell them, you offer food, drink, etc.)*

2. Connect heart to heart by crossing the devotional threshold. You must fall in love using transrational (beyond logic) devotion. *(Make this a heartfelt connection. This moves _____ from a historical figure or intellectual thought into a living presence. What would it feel like if_____ were here with me now?)*

3. Sit quietly in mutual awareness. *(Enjoy the now moment, enjoy the company of the beloved, soak up the love, be in the field of love)*

4. Communicate back and forth. *(Allow all your senses to be present, stay aware of incoming: words, pictures, feelings, physical touch)*

5. Resting as Infinite Being. *(Because once you become connected to the Divine, you can't help but know yourself as infinite too. This is about merging with the Divine.)*

Should you like to be guided in this process, below is link to a meditation I created for you to try: https://www.youtube.com/watch?v=2hxJGuvWRnA

(Worksheet 10)
Ponder and answer the following. Do the roles in your life define who you are? Do the roles help you to feel accomplished, successful, important, or give you a sense of belonging? Are these roles truly what you have come here, to this incarnation, to be? Do any of these roles engender feelings of shame, disappointment, or failure because you aren't living up to the expectations of others or yourself? Who are you, especially if you let go of your roles? Write your thoughts below in the lens as you see yourself:

My Roles: What are they?
How do I perceive myself by
what I do?

(Q4) In what areas are you acting on the outside that is not the truth on the inside?

(Worksheet 11)

But don't ask yourself if you are a racist, because your ego more than likely needs to protect and defend you. Your ego will say, "No, of course I am not racist. It's not who I am." But these are the types of questions to ask because they allow you to start a nonthreatening internal dialogue about your beliefs, while determining if the beliefs are even yours or someone else's. Do you feel you are more deserving than someone else? Do you think you have to get what's yours at the expense of someone else? Do you think your kids deserve a better education than someone else's kid? Do you think you should earn more money than someone who is an immigrant? Do you think working for an African American or Latin or Asian manager is acceptable? Do you call a woman darling or sweetheart?

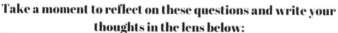

Take a moment to reflect on these questions and write your thoughts in the lens below:

(Table 2)

Let's be even more specific. Your way of communicating with yourself and others will completely change by following these simple reminders:

1. Ask questions: And get clarity, don't jump to conclusions, separate the facts from fiction. So here is the lesson–*ask more questions*! Don't get carried away in your own head about what is going on for the other person–*stop* and ask the question. Seek understanding in your relationships and conversations. I have to remind myself of this all the time, because assuming is a habit that we all form and it is a tough one to break. Assumptions are fast, easy, and they feel good because they are based on your own version of the truth. But the catch is, you aren't always right—sorry to disappoint you. Sure, sometimes our assumptions are bang-on but more often than not, they aren't.

2. Listen: Are you really listening to the person talking? Are you misinterpreting what they are saying? Are you finishing other's sentences? Sometimes we only hear and see what we want to hear and see. Take a moment to be present. Find that voice of yours and then respond with "I want to check out what I think you have said." Repeat that back to them.

3. Give yourself a break: This is life-changing work; therefore, give yourself a break. Be gentle with yourself. Sometimes we take three steps forward and then two back, but keep moving forward. Be comfortable in saying, "I don't know"—especially to stop making up stuff in your head.

4. Practice, practice, and practice.

(Table 3)
Your inner critic is usually an internalized negative voice, while your wisdom voice is inspired from divinity. If you don't discern the difference, then more often than not you will be tuning into your inner critic's voice. A few distinctions between inner critic and wisdom:

Inner Critic Voice or Thoughts	Wisdom Voice or Thoughts
Blaming, Shaming, Guilt-ridden	Accepting, Loving
Mean or Sarcastic	Hopeful and Full of Possibilities
Constricting	Expansive
Punitive Parent	Individuated Self

(Worksheet 12)

When you hear your inner critic, there are some steps you can take. Write your inner critic's thought here:

Then work through steps 1-5 in either the cognitive model or the psychospiritual model

Silencing Inner Critic By Dr. Koch Cognitive Behavior Model	Silencing Inner Critic Rev. Sheree's Model
1. Is the thought rational—scientifically provable?	1. Pay attention and tune in to your thoughts.
2. Feelings—does it make me feel the way I want to?	2. Name it.
3. Goals—does it achieve any short- / long-term goals?	3. Call it out.
4. Probable harm—is this going to cause me probable harm?	4. Love it.
5. Conflict—is it leading to internal or external conflict?	5. Release it.

(Q5) Whatever the situation, how is this *for* me?

(Worksheet 13)
So if you are struggling coming to terms with gifts from your family, I'll help you get started by suggesting a few and you finish:

Gifts from my parents: Add the gifts you received to this list and cross out the ones that don't apply

LIFE

SHELTER

ARTISTIC TALENTS

HOME

FOOD

SENSE OF HUMOR

EDUCATION

SIBLINGS

CLOTHING

STYLE

(Q6) What would you give to not be at war with anyone or anything? To create a world where there is enough for everyone, where no one needs to go without, and each person is valued and loved?

(Q7) "Is this what I really believe about myself, or is it something someone else has told me, something I have internalized as myself?" If the answer is "This isn't who I am," then what new belief system will you create about yourself?

(Q8) What are you waiting for?

(Q9) Are you ready to step into your power and your greatness? If so, write down specific actions and steps you will take.

Want To Go Deeper?

Should you want to take this work to the next level, you can contact me at info@preachitsister.com. For more information you can visit my website at PreachItSister.com and sign up for my newsletter to find out latest events, happenings, and discounts.

Some of my services are:
- Keynote Speaker
- Online Classes
- Online Group Discussions
- One-on-one Spiritual Direction
- Leading Experiential Workshops
- Spiritual Community/Church Guest Speaker

Made in the USA
Middletown, DE
15 September 2019